John

DREAMER

BUILDER

COLLECTOR

LEGACY

OF THE

CIRCUS

KING

Ringling

THE JOHN & MABLE RINGLING MUSEUM OF ART
THE STATE ART MUSEUM OF FLORIDA
5401 Bay Shore Road, Sarasota, Florida 34243

Published in conjunction with the Exhibition

John Ringling, Dreamer - Builder - Collector

The John & Mable Ringling Museum of Art

19 January — 28 December 1997

Generous Support for the Exhibition & Publication has been provided by:
The State of Florida, Department of State, Sandra B. Mortham, Secretary of State,
Division of Cultural Affairs and the Florida Arts Council; the Sarasota County Tourist
Development Tax through the Board of County Commissioners, the Tourist
Development council and the Sarasota County Arts Council; and RISCORP, the Season
Sponsor for the Ringling Museum.

Project Director & Editor	Mark Ormond
Project Coordinator & Editor	Aaron De Groft
Editor	Gene Ray
Designer	Golden Barton, Inc.
Printer	Ryan Creative Printing
Printed In	Hong Kong

The John & Mable Ringling Museum of Art Foundation is a private, fully incorporated,
nonprofit entity established to support the programs, activities, and staff of the Museum.

INTERNATIONAL STANDARD BOOK NUMBER   0-916758-36-2
LIBRARY OF CONGRESS CATALOG CARD NUMBER   96-77907

Table of Contents

Foreword

It is a rare moment in our lives, much less in the life of an institution such as The John and Mable Ringling Museum of Art, that we take time to reflect on our past. This is just such an occasion, as we celebrate fifty years of state ownership as the art museum of the people of Florida. It is time to take stock of the extraordinary art collection and museum that John Ringling left at his death in 1936 to the State of Florida, along with Cà d'Zan, the residence that he and his wife, Mable, built overlooking Sarasota Bay. This gift was accepted by the State in 1946.

John Ringling, Dreamer - Builder - Collector tells the story of John Ringling's vision for Sarasota, how he assembled his collection in a remarkably short period from 1925 to 1931, and in 1930 opened one of the most beautiful museums in the world. It may be surprising that John Ringling, the circus king, should seek to become a collector and connoisseur of art. Creating an art museum of this scope in Florida provided the cultural amenity that Sarasota was otherwise sadly lacking to aid Ringling in developing his extensive real estate interests. Collecting was an occupation proper to a gentleman of means, and founding a museum was a civic gesture that could perpetuate the names of John and Mable Ringling.

John Ringling educated himself with the help of dealers such as Julius Böhler, and assembled a sizable personal library of art books. He often exercised his own judgment in making purchases at auction and from dealers. In a telegram he sent to Julius Böhler in 1929, Ringling wrote: "Wallace picture practically the same except shadeings on hands are more of a brown and fingers on right hand little wider spread and blue dress little darker shade. Altogether Munich picture looks to me like finer quality." These are words of a person who trained himself to look closely and make fine distinctions. The quality of the collection bears witness to this accomplishment.

These essays accompany a series of exhibitions and educational programs that have been organized to celebrate John Ringling's legacy. We could not appreciate the full extent of this legacy without the extensive restoration of the interior of the art museum funded by the State Legislature that was undertaken under the direction of my predecessor, Dr. Laurence J. Ruggiero. Much of the history of John Ringling and the Museum would remain hidden without the organization of the Museum Archives initiated by Lynell A. Morr, former Museum Librarian, and completed by Deborah W. Walk, Curator of the Circus Museum and Historical Resources. Mark Ormond, Deputy Director for Collections and Programs, has led the team preparing the publication, exhibitions and related programs, and the funding for these ambitious ventures owes much to the energy of Dr. Susan Brainerd, Deputy Director for Development and Marketing. Thanks to these and to the many other staff, volunteers and supporters acknowledged in these pages, we can tell the story of John Ringling, dreamer, builder and collector, and look forward to preserving and building upon his legacy to the people of Florida.

Dr. David Ebitz
Director

Acknowledgments

In the fall of 1994, I proposed to David Ebitz, the Director, the idea of organizing an exhibition that would look at the history of the formation of the collection and an accompanying publication that would encourage new research to uncover information about how John Ringling actually went about building the collection and the museum. In less than two years we are going to press with this publication. In addition to thanking David and the Board of Trustees for their encouragement and support there are many individuals who have made this document possible.

The authors of the essays, whom I list in the order they appear in this volume, I thank for the considerable new research they have undertaken and for all their other contributions. David Weeks adapted much research he completed several years ago but was unable to use in his biography of Ringling. Heather Ewing who recently co-authored a history of the Smithsonian Institution took on the Herculean task of researching all the newspapers and periodicals that might have mentioned Ringling for the period 1924-1936. Eric Zafran was challenged by the gift to the museum archives of the papers kept by Julius Böhler located by his grandson in Munich who mailed them to us in the autumn of 1995. Eric has also written another essay focused on the collection of Baroque paintings. Lee De Groft assisted by Deborah Walk and Jan Silberstein created an extraordinary essay and a database on the history of John Ringling's activities in and out of the auction house. Linda McKee relocated over five hundred volumes from Ringling's original collection of books that had been dispersed throughout the library and composed an insightful view of the printed matter that informed and educated the collector. Deborah Krohn followed leads to the files of the Metropolitan in New York and sources in Paris to uncover much of the mystery of the Gavet Collection and its journey to Sarasota. And finally, after twice delivering papers at the museum on the Astor Rooms, Michael Conforti will see his research published. His work has stimulated a further, thorough, on-site investigation into the history of these two rooms and has led to the discovery in storage of the ceiling painting to the library.

Many individuals locally and throughout the country have been helpful in gathering materials, information and photography. Appreciation is extended to: Anne Bulin, The Rhode Island Historical Society; Stav Burnbaum, Bettman Archive, New York; Debora Cohen, TIME LIFE Syndication, New York; Cynthia Duval; Everett Fahy; Alan Fern, National Portrait Gallery, Washington, D.C.; Françoise Hack; Constance Holcomb; Myrtle Lane; Gail Levy; Kern Maas; Nicole McCarren; Michael McDonough; Paul Miller, Preservation Society of Newport County, Newport, Rhode Island; Dick Mottino; Lila Niemi; James Peck; Earl A Powell, III, National Gallery of Art, Washington, D.C.; Edna Rosenbaum; and Peter Tomory.

The entire staff of the museum has contributed enormously to this publication in each area of their expertise. The Division of Collections & Programs took the lead in this publication and everyone is to be thanked. Appreciation is extended to Susan Brainerd, Deputy Director, Development & Marketing, Gary Lamm, Deputy Director, Finance & Administration and Tom Johnson, Assistant Director for Security and

Visitors Services and all their staffs for their ongoing contributions to the success of this publication. Special thanks to Linda Chessler, Barbara Linick, Janice Maginness, Myrtle Myers, Robert McComb and Dawn Saunders.

The specific requirements of a publication such as this depends on a focused team that deserves appreciation: Arden McKennee for proofreading and copy editing, Terry Shank for new photography, Mike Everson for custom photography, Michael Golden for the design, Gene Ray for editing. Special mention must be made of Jacqueline Ansboury who assisted me with innumerable details, Michele Scalera for conservation issues, Ed Amatore for assistance in registration materials, Ron McCarty for research assistance and photography, Bob Huntress for details of object preparation, Jan Silberstein for her friendship and dedication as a volunteer member of the curatorial staff for over twenty years and for more than doubling the number of her hours to see this project to completion, Linda McKee for extensive assistance with interlibrary research and queries, Deborah Walk for exhaustive searches, planning, coordination and technological resource management solutions and Lee De Groft for organizing the Böhler papers, endless tracking of new leads and searches. Aaron De Groft joined the staff less than one year ago. I am grateful for his dedication and attention to accuracy in research, remarkable sense of humor, skills of diplomacy, mastery of untold complications in computer software and his indefatigable attention to coordinating all aspects of this project.

Mark Ormond
Deputy Director
Collections & Programs

Introduction

To set foot on the property of the State Art Museum of Florida is to wonder in amazement about the person who not only conceived to build such historically referential buildings but also to assemble a collection of thousands of works of art. Walking northwest from the art museum across the magnificent grounds a glint of the Museum of the Circus lodges in the corner of my right eye. Directly on axis with my path is the rose garden and beyond, the door leading into the kitchen of Cà d' Zan.

In 1926, John Ringling might have taken this route, after leaving a meeting with his museum architect John Phillips, walking toward the house where inside Mable Ringling was discussing details of her "House of John" soon to be completed by architect Dwight James Baum. Ringling may have been contemplating the disposition of a case shipment of paintings soon arriving from New York by rail. He too, may have been briefly distracted by the thought of some issue regarding his Circus that in the late twenties was becoming less a part of his focus and his driving ambition than his desire to build an extraordinary museum for art, a memorial to be called the John and Mable Ringling Museum of Art. The Museum of the Circus now on the grounds and an important part of the complex was not part of his original plan and would come later in 1948, but that is another story.

This publication **John Ringling, Dreamer - Builder - Collector** is a collection of essays that begins to answer many of the questions that have arisen since the museum was acquired by the State of Florida from John Ringling at his death on December 2, 1936.

While there have been numerous and significant scholarly catalogues on aspects of the collection by authors including: Suida (1949), Tomory (1976), Wilson (1980) and Duval (1983), none have been published since Janson (1986). This new publication investigates not only issues of Ringling's motivation to build a museum in the southeast corner of his 37 acre property on Sarasota Bay but also who and what informed his decisions in acquiring a great collection of paintings. Mable Ringling gave only one known press interview and quotations by John about his projects in Sarasota scarcely appear. To our knowledge no diaries or substantial correspondence of the Ringlings exists. Each author was asked to approach an aspect of the formation of the collection and building of the museum from a different perspective. Our intention was to permit not only the museum visitor choosing a book to add more information to their on-site experience but also the curious reader making a bookstore purchase on the Lido in Venice to come to a better understanding and appreciation of John Ringling's contribution to the people of the State of Florida and the world.

Mark Ormond

The Dream Realized

The Building of the Museum

by David Weeks

The John and Mable Ringling Museum of Art is essentially a statement of John Ringling's personal passion and tastes in the realm of fine art — a statement that has endured undiminished for 50 years of public ownership. It belongs to the small class of elegant American art museums conceived, financed, and installed by a single individual. But unlike several others of that class, the Ringling Museum was not restricted by the donor to house only the collector's original bequest. The terms of Ringling's gift provided for maintaining and expanding the collection, thus freeing it from the frozen moment of its origin. Still, Ringling's driving ambition and imagination is as evident today as it was in 1925, when he first announced his intention to build a memorial museum.

Figure 1. Photograph of John Ringling with his dog, "Tell," on the front steps of Cà d'Zan, circa 1928. Photograph: UPI / Corbis - Bettmann.

It was Ringling's good fortune to be assisted by a talented architect, John H. Phillips, and a mentor-dealer, Julius Böhler of Munich and Lucerne. The building Phillips designed for him to house the museum — the architect's most important work — is itself a monumental statement. Phillips' design shows an exact understanding of the Ringlings' love and admiration for the culture of the Italian Renaissance. Phillips himself spent most of his fellowship study in Italy. In evoking the Italian grace and spirit, he could call freely upon his own experience without resorting to mere imitation. And Böhler's knowledge and tastes contributed materially not only to the strengths and scope of the collection, but also to the decoration of the building.

Nature was surely Phillips' foremost ally, for the open blue sky and the sub-tropical, park-like setting still lend an airy charm to the massive villa. Rarely have the enthusiasms and skills of a partnership resulted in such a beautiful unified complex of structures and landscape, combined with an interior worthy of the rich and colorful collection. This is, indeed, a museum that represents the

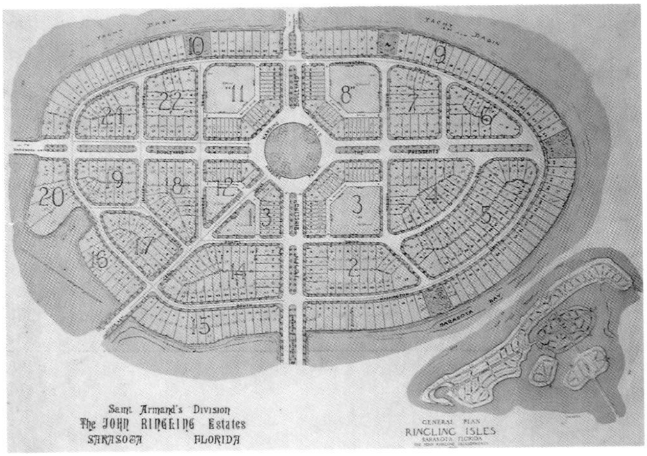

Figure 2. Plat number 1, Ringling Isles, currently known as St. Armand's, one of John Ringling's numerous Sarasota developments.

past and its great heritage. But at the end of a time line that reaches back to the mid-fourteenth century, it addresses itself to the present as well.

Ringling was at the peak of his fortune in 1925. In that year his Sarasota investments and influence reached their widest scope. Then 59 years old, Ringling had behind him a many-sided career. Each stage of his accumulation of wealth and possessions reflected his intellectual qualities of initiative, imagination and business acumen. The same qualities are apparent in his bold move into the international art market, where he advanced from novice to collector-connoisseur in a remarkably short span of years. Ringling's personality and character were also behind his domination of the national market in outdoor entertainment — a notoriously volatile industry. While associates and competitors alike found the showman egocentric and acquisitive, it must be said that such qualities are highly useful and hardly uncommon among art collectors.

Few art museums in the nation retain, as has this one, an original collection undiluted by subsequent gifts and bequests of whole collections of differing character. The Circus Galleries, added to the Museum complex in 1948, increased the public's pleasure, but had no significant impact on the Art museum. As a consequence, the collection — its Baroque content unique in American museums — still reflects Ringling's personality and personal preferences. William Suida, while at work on the first complete catalogue in 1941, wrote that the museum "has a prominent, in some respects a unique place, among American museums.... the personal taste of John Ringling is fully recognizable; therefore, the museum has the charm of a strong individuality."[1]

For the first few years of the 1920s, Ringling's idea of establishing a museum remained an undefined vision. But by 1925 he had formed in his mind the outline of his intended gift to the people of Florida. Occasionally he referred to the proposed museum as a resource, an art center for the South in general, for there was no major museum for public enjoyment in the Southeastern states. The idea of putting together an art collection was scarcely new. For some 25 years he had been buying works of art. The intriguing glow of prosperity generated by the Florida land boom seemed certain to bring new wealth to Sarasota. The time was right for acting on his dream of founding a museum on his Gulfside estate. Many would find it difficult or even impossible to reconcile his new incarnation as a collector of Old Masters with his renowned show-business background.

In Sarasota, Ringling was perceived as a rich and influential leader; whatever he chose to build would enhance that image. A man who loved life and action as well as the pleasures and beautiful objects that riches could buy, he would not have been satisfied with anything less than a massive museum building — the largest located south of New York's Metropolitan Museum of Art (fig. 4). Long galleries, huge canvases, an air of splendor, even magnificence: these were the kinds of features he desired.

Figure 3. View of the entrance façade of Cà d'Zan, circa 1928. The front car is one of Ringling's numerous Pierce-Arrows. Photograph: UPI / Corbis - Bettmann.

While he rarely spoke in public about his personal interests, Ringling's occasional statements about his plans for a museum indicate a three-fold aim. First, he planned the proposed bequest as a memorial to himself and his wife, Mable. Their names are permanently carved into stone on the frieze over the Museum entrance (pl. 1). Understandably, a wish to be remembered would be foremost. Ringling's passion to be conspicuously successful had been shaped in the 1870s and impelled by the unbridled ambition of his circus-partner brothers.

His other aims were less intensely personal and more pragmatic. He wished to give the people of the southern states an opportunity to study art without leaving the region. Friends Mayor Jimmy Walker of New York City and Mayor Frank Hague of Jersey City urged him to gain wider exposure by establishing his museum in the metropolitan area. He rejected their advice, citing his affection for Sarasota as the deciding factor. Further, he purposely avoided following current fashion and tastes in assembling his collection. He wished, he said, to

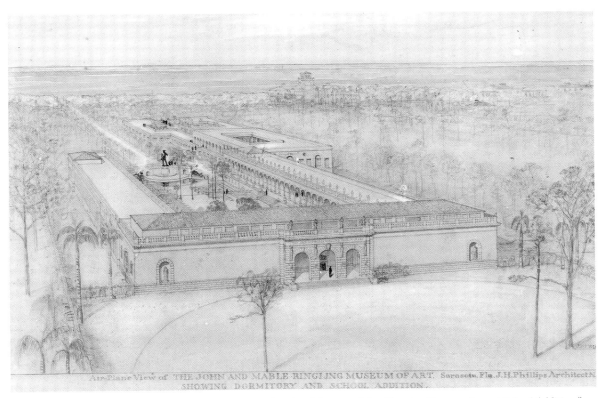

Figure 4. J.H. Phillips, "Air Plane View of John and Mable Ringling Museum of Art, Showing Dormatories and School Addition," 1928. Pencil/watercolor, 11 x 23 inches.

Figure 5. J.H. Phillips, "View of Hall of Architecture and Sculpture Casts," circa 1926. Pencil/watercolor, 10 x 16 1/2 inches.

Figure 6. Installation of Chiurazzi bronze copy of Michelangelo's *David* on the bridge across the Museum courtyard, circa 1929.

Figure 8. View looking east down south loggia under construction, circa 1928-29. Note marble fountain basin and brick support of pier system.

Figure 7. View of north wing and courtyard under construction, looking east, circa 1928-29.

THE DREAM REALIZED

develop a collection as nearly universal as opportunities and purse would allow. He came closest to achieving that aim in the diversity of Italian schools represented. For Sarasota in particular he saw the presence of a well-rounded museum as an enduring cultural asset which would enrich the community and ensure a quality of life uniquely different from the showy resorts of the East Coast.

A third, equally compelling purpose shared by John and Mable Ringling was their intent to found a school of visual art as an important adjunct to the museum. The school was intended to occupy a large share of the museum building as an extended north wing (fig. 4). The picture galleries, holding representative examples from important periods and schools of European painting and sculpture, would nurture and inspire young artists. Mable, pleased with the allusions to Italian art and architecture in Phillips' Renaissance villa, especially regarded the museum as a laboratory for the study of Italian culture. Its dual function would be to disseminate formal learning and to encourage the appreciation and production of art. The entire complex would reflect its dedication to enjoyment.

In what may have been the noblest aspect of their museum concept, both Ringlings envisioned the influence of the Museum and the School of Art as a strong magnet, drawing established artists to Sarasota. There, painters and sculptors might take advantage of an ambiance — a certain luminosity of sunlight and glistening water — not unlike that of Venice. And perhaps a "Sarasota School" of painting would emerge to rival the nation's indigenous Hudson River School and its interval of illumination. "Perhaps in time," Ringling suggested, "the School would equal the Barbizon School of France."[2]

The Creation of an Italian Villa for Art

John H. Phillips was not nationally known, but he proved to be an ideal choice for the museum architect. Fellowship study in Italy had made him an Italophile devoted, as were the Ringlings, to that culture's Renaissance and Baroque splendors. First trained as an engineer, Phillips worked with architectural firms in Madison, Wisconsin, Chicago and New York City before opening his own studio. He had done his best work as a team member, sharing the design of ponderous stone structures that included New York's Grand Central Station and the central block of the Metropolitan Museum of Art. These were challenges of a different order from that posed by the spacious Ringling estate on Sarasota Bay.

Phillips first met the Ringlings while working on a small Italianate villa on the adjoining estate of Ralph Caples. At Mable's request, Phillips designed for her a Venetian guest house located next to the new Ringling home, Cà d'Zan. The cottage suggested homes found on the smaller Venetian islands such as Burano, and it also prefigured certain details of the art museum to come. In the process, Phillips and the Ringlings became a compatible team, mutually confident and ready to start on an unprecedented project — a seaside museum in Southwest Florida.

Figure 9. J.H. Phillips, "View from Italian Room," circa 1927. Drawing, 10 x 13 1/2 inches. Note tall window right piercing north wall.

Prior to his first purchase of museum-quality paintings, Ringling asked John Phillips early in 1925 to prepare a preliminary plan for a museum. One month later Phillips returned from New York with a cardboard model. Delighted with its Renaissance style and ready to draw down some of his accumulated capital, Ringling urged his newly-commissioned architect to proceed with specific designs (pls. 2, 3 and 4). Phillips had already decided on a great Tuscan villa. He had ample time to study precedents, for two years passed before a design was agreed upon and a site selected at the southeast corner of the Ringling estate. In the interval, Florida's land boom had collapsed. Ringling's Ritz Carlton Hotel venture folded, leaving a ghostly, unfinished hulk; his investment had become a total loss. Masses of Italian architectural relics and statues purchased for the hotel and its gardens were now made available for Phillips to install in the museum building and grounds.

Decorative material purchased in the summer of 1925 — most in Venice and the remainder

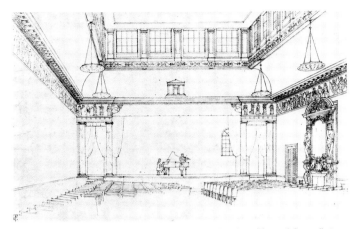

Figure 10. J.H. Phillips, "View of Auditorium Looking Toward Stage," circa 1927. Drawing, 11 x 14 inches. Note that in the actual construction of this room, now gallery 21, the marble fireplace and sculptural overmantle were sited on the east wall, rather than on the west as indicated in the drawing.

in Rome and Naples — arrived by barge from Tampa or by ship from Miami. Whenever possible, shipments were documented as antiques by American consuls in Italy to permit duty-free entry. Shipments mixed old and new — new cast-stone statues and columns, antique marble wall fountains, marble doorways, and modern castings of familiar classical sculptures.

Two large fountains, and copies of important Italian sculpture, were to ornament the court. One, a reproduction of the Isolotto fountain by Giovanni da Bologna (Jean Boulogne) in the Boboli gardens in Florence, represents Oceanus and the three great rivers — Nile, Euphrates, and Ganges. The other is a copy of the Rome monument to Pope Alexander VII. A third heroic sculpture — more than 16 feet in height — for the museum court was a bronze casting of Michelangelo's *David* (fig. 6), ordered on the first Italian buying trip Ringling made with Böhler. It was cast at the Chiurazzi foundry in Naples from the same forms used in 1874 to make three bronze copies. All this material awaited decisions for placement in and around the museum.

In his final plans, Phillips incorporated fifteenth to eighteenth century design details from Renaissance and Baroque buildings to achieve an effect of balance and harmony. His Italian sketches provided inspiration for a design that suggests several important sources, including the larger courtyard of Donato Bramante's Santa Maria delle Grazie (1480-1490) in Milan. While the Ringling museum is not a reproduction of one single Italian building, it is clear that well-known works by several of Italy's most talented architects provided Phillips with inspiration for aspects of his design. For example, the museum loggia and a three-sided open court, show traces of both the elegant court by Luciano Laurana at the Palazzo Ducale in Urbino (1465-1479) and Filippo Brunelleschi's great rhythmic arches at the Ospedali degli Innocenti (1419-1424) in Florence. The loggia's U-shaped range of semi-round arches and slender pink columns contribute to the formal dignity and elegance of the court and garden (figs. 7 and 8). The deceptive simplicity of Phillips' court and loggia design conceals exceedingly complex structural details. Böhler, in a much later recollection, claimed it was his own suggestion to mount the 76 cast-stone statues on the roof line balustrade — a feature found in several of Andrea Palladio's most striking villas in Vicenza, but one more common in Baroque than in Renaissance buildings. Phillips used steel beams cantilevered over the loggia to give support to the roof and to bear the weight of the statues.

The loggia is one of two scenes of architectural drama that Phillips achieved with the Museum design. The other is the east facade where the central mass is faced in rusticated pink and gray blocks of cast stone, emphasized by three great, open arches ornamented by white marble caryatids and a massive cartouche above the keystone. From the ample supply of decorative objects, Phillips selected two *Furietti* centaurs to flank the marble steps. These were modern bronze castings of Hellenistic originals found at Hadrian's country villa at Tivoli, outside Rome. While one represents the bitterness of passion in old age, the other smiles with the joyful passion of youth. Above the roof line balustrade and against the blue Florida sky, four monumental statues representing Music, Sculpture, Architecture and Painting add heroic grandeur to the entrance.

Many of the interior and exterior decorative materials came from auctions in New York and Europe. One gallery is distinguished by a beamed Renaissance ceiling delicately embellished with soft colors and gold leaf designed by C.R. Renshaw, one of Phillips' assistants. This gallery also features unique turquoise and gilt wood wainscot panels that were originally cabinet doors in the library of the historic Villa Palmieri near Florence (fig. 9). This library was renowned as the room where Giovanni Boccaccio, who lived in the Villa to escape the plague, wrote his *Decameron* in 1352. Two galleries with vaulted ceilings were designed to display the earliest works in the collection — late Gothic panels and what were then called primitives.

Ringling's first purchases from Böhler in Naples were the origins of his museum-quality collection. These were supplemented by his purchases at the 1926 sales of the Astor home in New York, which included four moderately fine paintings from the more than 100 that hung in the great ballroom-picture gallery. He also paid $10,000 for two seventeenth century Brussels tapestries, among the few then owned by American collectors.[3]

Before being demolished, the massive French Renaissance chateau designed for Caroline

Figure 11. J.H. Phillips, drawing for decoration of crypt, view looking south, 1928, 14 x 10 inches.

Figure 12. Black and white photograph by Irving Underhill, NYC, of bronze doorway purchased by John Ringling and integrated by Phillips into the crypt under the Museum bridge.

Schermerhorn Astor by Richard Morris Hunt in 1895 was stripped of its finery. Ringling bought two paneled rooms, a cream and gold salon and a library in dark oak and parcel gilt. The library, with its attached small kitchen, was planned as a reception room for the museum, suggesting that Ringling's vision for the institution included social functions as well as a cultural role. The elegance of the two Astor rooms, connected to an array of picture galleries, would surely meet Ringling's desire for an elite setting. Another important purchase was the great wrought bronze inner entrance screen from the Fifth Avenue side of the Astor home. Its finely worked doors and wings, or side lights are fully thirteen feet across and bear on its lintel a salamander cartouche alluding to the French Valois kings at Blois. The whole massive assembly became the main museum entrance in the east facade.

The Museum is Established

Almost two years after Phillips had presented his initial model, the charter of June 16, 1927, established the Ringling Museum as an institution. John and Mable Ringling were named as officers, while Böhler became curator, a post he held until the museum was conveyed to the state of Florida.[4] Construction began under the firm of Hageman and Harris of Chicago and Tampa. Work was suspended almost at once, however, and only resumed in late summer. On this second start, construction began at the west end of the north wing. A new contractor, Ringling's friend Lyman Chase of Alpine, New Jersey, assumed direction. In the winter of 1927 and again in 1928, several hundred craftsmen and decorators from the circus winter quarters expanded the local work force. Structural walls were of interlocking hollow tile covered with "oriental plaster" (stucco) colored an apricot pink. Interior walls were of plaster applied directly to the tile surface. In an ill-advised economy measure, lathe and water seal were eliminated, leading to delayed, devastating effects. All balustrades, cornices, and copings were made locally at the Binz Cast Stone Company whose offices were at nearby Sapphire Shores.

Phillips designed the galleries to be arranged *enfilade*, thus eliminating the need for a corridor. At each gallery entrance he placed flanking columns or important architectural doorways.

The largest gallery, facing the Rubens gallery across the main entrance, was planned for use as an auditorium as well as a place to display tapestries and paintings of "epic proportion" (fig. 10). For this prominent gallery Ringling provided an immense marble fireplace and chimney piece and a matching door frame. A white marble frieze below the clerestory conveyed a classical appearance. Overall, Phillips' use of space and light created an airy ambiance befitting its sun-lit site on the Gulf. There were no dim passages nor dark stairways to rob the museum of its charm. Phillips planned innovative electric heat — the first public building to be so designed — but his system was never completely installed. For lighting, he relied on long windows in place of Ringling's preferred skylights. Florida's climate and its frequent violent storms made overhead glass unsafe. The window openings were later bricked over during the renovation undertaken by the second director, Kenneth Donahue.

At the end of 1928 the building was substantially complete. One of several add-on tasks called for Phillips to design an elaborate crypt in the curved gallery under the bridge between the two wings. A finely carved alabaster screen would protect marble sarcophagi sculpted in Europe for John and Mable — not unlike memorials to royalty and princes of the Church (figs. 11 and 12). After Mable's death in June of 1929, Ringling decided not to complete the costly and opulent tomb. Instead, he wished to select a burial site elsewhere on the estate.[5] His wish was not realized until 1992 when a gift from Henry Ringling North enabled the museum trustees to set aside a plot for the remains of John and Mable Ringling and John's sister, Ida Ringling North.

After three years of rapid buying Ringling had accumulated the greater part of his art collection. While most of the paintings were stored in New York City warehouses, some remained in Europe. There, Böhler supervised arrangements for cleaning and repairing panels, canvases and frames. A number of the finer, even spectacular frames that are currently seen in the galleries were purchased with a view to adding dignity and splendor to the collection. For the large Rubens cartoons, new wood frames were made in Germany and shipped to Sarasota for installation inside the engaged plaster frames of the specially designed gallery.[6]

On three occasions Ringling made major purchases that helped to define his collection and measurably broadened the nature of the Museum. In 1928, he bought almost the entire Newport

Marble House collection of Gothic and proto-Renaissance treasures — paintings, jewelry, faience, furniture, and a whole treasury of liturgical objects. William K. Vanderbilt had bought the collection from Emile Gavet, a French collector. (For more on the Gavet collection, see Deborah Krohn's essay.) Also in 1928 Ringling added a wholly disparate component to his collections. He bought more than 2300 archaic and antique objects from the Luigi Palma di Cesnola Cypriote collection auctioned by the Metropolitan Museum of Art. In a plan never realized, Ringling intended to house these relics of early Western art in a separate building.

In the following year, 1929, the Earl of Yarborough's important art collection was sold at Christie's. In a move curious for one who took the role of art collector seriously, Ringling bought — among some 20 canvases that day — a discredited "Rembrandt." In a jubilant telegram to Böhler listing his purchases, he added "For sport I paid 550 Guineas for the so-called Rembrandt Old Lady."[7] Whatever sport he expected to derive must have seemed worth 550 guineas. The picture, then titled *A Woman with Folded Hands* had been in several collections in the U.S. and abroad. It was never listed in a Ringling inventory catalogue, yet John Ringling was not a man to lightly invest almost $3000 for sport. The canvas was a good example of the many "Rembrandts" that found their way into private collections and museums before science came to the aid of connoisseurs.

The question of a public opening was becoming an issue in part because premature publicity had promised access when the galleries were far from ready. In 1928 *Art News* (generally favorable to Ringling) had remarked on the "mysterious" nature of the still unopened Sarasota museum. Florida's Gulf Coast was far from the metropolitan centers where collectors, dealers, and critics held forth. Moreover, public and professional curiosity was aroused by press accounts of a collection said to contain "the world's finest paintings." At the same time, equally uninformed critics claimed Ringling owned nothing but copies and works of indifferent quality.

Nothing short of a public opening could dispel unfounded praise or mean-spirited canards. Clearly, if the museum were to achieve recognized status, a carefully prepared catalogue was essential to establish the authority of the collection. Several examples suggest that Ringling gained a measure of exposure by lending occasionally to exhibitions mounted by prestigious commercial galleries. As early as December, 1925, the Reinhardt Galleries in New York showed Bernardino Luini's *Madonna and Child with St. Sebastian and St. Roche* (pl. 5) — one of Ringling's earliest purchases. In October of 1929, the Kleinberg Galleries in New York opened an exhibition of early Flemish paintings. Among the lenders were major museums and prominent collectors such as Andrew Mellon and John D. Rockefeller, Jr. Ringling's friend Albert Keller sent Adriaen Isenbrandt's *Donor and St. John the Baptist*. Ringling sent three paintings: Cornelis van Cleve's *Nativity*, Isenbrant's *Descent from the Cross*, and Jan Mostaert's *Portrait of a Lady with a Standard*. In 1930, he loaned his two Rembrandts, *St. John* and *Portrait of a Woman*, to the Detroit Institute of the Arts. These loans were important precedents, establishing Ringling's willingness to

Figure 13. J.H. Phillips, "View from Main Entrance Towards Rubens Gallery," circa 1927. Drawing, 14 x 10 inches Note two columns flanking passage from gallery 1 to gallery 2 in drawing were eliminated in actual execution of design.

participate in exhibitions. Curiously, his first contact with A. Everett Austin, the Museum's first director, was through Austin's request to show several of Ringling's Italian Baroque paintings at the Wadsworth Atheneum in Hartford, Connecticut.

Ringling opened the museum for one day on March 31, 1930. Invited guests and the public viewed the entire collection for the first time. With the paintings triple-hung, salon style, the crowded walls of the galleries displayed more than 500 works — about double the number currently shown. Austin described the initial display as a "kind of glorified storage warehouse."[8] So eager were the local residents and nearby communities to see the much-publicized treasures that the throng of visitors, herded by Sarasota Boy Scouts, exceeded the total number of Sarasota's population. The majestic impact Ringling had intended was heightened in the first two galleries by the rich color and energetic power of the two tapestries and the four cartoons from Rubens' *Triumph of the Eucharist* series.

Almost a year later, on March 2, 1931, the museum was opened for one week. Ringling's frustration at the absence of a catalogue led to an abrupt closing. The topic had become a matter of some tension, though without expressed rancor, between Ringling and Böhler (see Eric Zafran's essay on the Ringling-Böhler correspondence in this volume). In part the delay arose from the poor quality of the photographs sent from Sarasota, made useless by the glare of sunlight reflected off the painted surface. Böhler, recognizing that his own reputation would suffer irreparable harm in Europe if a hasty and unscientific catalogue were released, rejected half of the photos.[9] Meanwhile, the single-copy inventory, supposedly safe in Böhler's keeping, was lost in the mail, or mislaid. It was never found or replaced. Böhler later prepared several partial lists by source, citing purchases from London or New York auction houses. But these were not complete. When an inventory was required a year later, not more than 350 titles were listed.[10]

Still, friends and applicants were the only visitors allowed into the museum. One friend who visited Ringling in 1932, publisher and writer Joe Mitchell Chappelle, described his guided tour. Ringling "knew details of every canvas...when, how, and where the art trophy was secured. He knew the value of each picture and just where the artist's signature was placed... a complete catalogue in his head."[11] Elsewhere in 1931, events of far-reaching importance were already in motion. The Great Depression was spreading in Europe. Financial straits soon intervened upon Ringling's and Böhler's enterprises. Ringling's collecting phase ended abruptly. As a device to resolve the catalogue dilemma, Böhler proposed that an early opening could be arranged with a sample catalogue of about 75 entries to satisfy critics for a time. Ringling failed to adopt the suggestion. It was the last opportunity. Böhler's catalogue was never completed, and no further action was taken during Ringling's lifetime.

Opening the Art School

Ringling was determined to honor the wish that he shared for so long with Mable to found a school of art. The latest idea of including it within a John Ringling University had become wholly untenable. Ringling no longer had the resources for a major venture in a field in which he had no experience. An alternative plan, to be minimally financed by Ringling, was proposed by President Ludd M. Spivey of Southern College in Lakeland. By joining the new school to the existing college, a new program could be created that would qualify graduates to teach in Florida schools. The school held a precarious position, however, for lacking the limited liability of a corporation, it exposed the faculty to personal liability in the event of fiscal failure. Nor was it governed by an independent board of trustees. Despite these flaws, the school was opened in a nearby hotel and dedicated with the museum at a joint ceremony on October 1, 1931.

Recognizing that further delays in a public opening of the museum would arouse unfriendly critics, Ringling announced that the museum would be permanently open beginning on January 17, 1932. There would be no admission fee, only a 25 cent charge for vehicles in the parking lot. The museum was still without a professional staff.[12] Böhler retained his title as curator but his visits to America became rarer as he struggled to keep his firm solvent in a stagnant art market. Thus the leaderless museum entered its first phase as an open gallery without the verifiable authority of a catalogue. Several months later Ringling fell permanently ill and in July of 1932 came under siege by his creditors. Most of his assets were pledged as collateral for a circus debt of nearly $2 million. All his art collection was transferred to a Delaware corporation he named the Rembrandt Corporation. Notwithstanding Ringling's claim to total ownership, the 100 shares were issued to an agent of his circus creditors.[13] The deepening Depression and the accompanying collapse of Ringling's fortune placed the Museum and his collection at serious risk. The illness that confined him in the summer of 1932 compounded his distress. His creditors had no use for the museum building, but they soon held the collection hostage to their loan. Alarmed by the possibility of a foreclosed museum, local and state officials levied retroactive property taxes as a device to establish a priority claim ahead of any private debt. Ringling quietly consulted Böhler about possibly selling a share of the collection in Europe with a view to later repurchasing the same or comparable works. He asked for an overall appraisal. Böhler named a figure of $4 million — about $1 million over cost.[14] Thus, when Ringling died on December 2, 1936, the museum and its collection were embroiled in an incredibly tangled estate. Ten years were required for the executors to sort out his affairs and deliver the museum and his home to the state of Florida as Ringling intended.

Early Perceptions of the Museum

A Worldview

Heather P. Ewing

In the spring of 1928, John Ringling appeared on the radar of the art world with his purchase of most of the lots in the Metropolitan Museum of Art's sale of "duplicates" or surplus objects from their Cypriote collection. These sculptures, dating from the eighth century B.C. to the first century A.D., had been chiefly collected in the 1870s by U.S. consul and later Director of the Metropolitan, Luigi Palma di Cesnola. An open auction of such a fine collection of antiquities had little precedent in the U.S. *Art News* hailed it as "unique," an "event that may represent a turning point in our understanding of ancient art."[1] Ringling acquired nearly three-quarters of all the offerings, paying the highest prices at the auction, and purchasing many of the finest pieces. As the most conspicuous purchaser at the sale, Ringling emerged as the owner of one of the largest collections of archaic Greek art outside the Metropolitan. Word of his plan to install the antiquities in their own building at his newly established art museum catapulted the circus owner into the spotlight as an art collector of note. Art journals, magazines and newspapers rushed to interview him, to be the first to tell the story of the creation of this unusual museum. The stories that followed, many featuring a photograph of the museum's majestic courtyard, tantalized readers with descriptions of a vast and superlative collection. The John and Mable Ringling Museum was proclaimed to house the finest collection in the South, set within an architectural framework reminiscent of those erected by the great turn-of-the-century collector-barons such as J.P. Morgan and Henry Clay Frick.

By the spring of 1928, Ringling's fantastical Italian Renaissance art palace on Florida's Gulf Coast — already three years in the making — was substantially complete. In retrospect, it is surprising that the creation of what was hailed as the "first great museum in the South"[2] had slipped by virtually unnoticed. There are a number of possible reasons for this oversight, including the remoteness of Sarasota from the art center of New York and Ringling's lack of professional ties to the museum establishment. His interest in large-scale Baroque art at a time in which it was very much

> *So quietly has Mr. Ringling done his collecting and his building that the news of the erection and establishment of this art museum comes like a bolt out of a clear sky.*
>
> — *American Magazine of Art, May 1928*

out of fashion and his abiding association with the circus world also seem crucial factors. For years, John Ringling had been making headlines as the head of the "Greatest Show On Earth." He was in people's minds the most prominent of the Ringling brothers, the builder of the largest circus in the world — not a likely candidate to assemble a serious art collection.

In 1925, when Ringling first embarked on his efforts to create a museum, he was at the pinnacle of his career as head of the Ringling Brothers-Barnum and Bailey Circus. He appeared on the cover of TIME magazine (fig. 14), when the circus' 1925 season opened in New York City without, for the first time, the daredevil lion and tiger acts. In keeping with the tradition of the circus as wholesome family fun that he and his brothers had established decades earlier, Ringling had decided that "carnivoras" would no longer perform under the big top. Echoing the public's wonder, the TIME article rhetorically asked who it was who had decided that "the fever of those who rock with thrills at wild animal acts is not very different from that of the demobilized centurions who howled in the Roman hippodromes..."[3] The answer was John Ringling, the "shrewdest" of the Brothers, lauded for his acquisition of three western railroads and his intimate knowledge of the business.

In 1925, Ringling's financial status had never been better. The financial acumen he had displayed in developing the giant circus corporation he also applied to the development of Sarasota, his elected home. Florida was experiencing the height of its land boom, with an enormous influx of new residents and real estate speculation. After over a decade in the town, Ringling was an active and commanding participant. He had acquired extensive property along the valuable islands across the bay and had devoted a great deal of resources to dredging and seawall construction to enable development. Most of his elaborate projects were nearing completion in 1925: the causeway to these island properties, the landscaping and development of resort-like communities on these islands, the Ritz Carlton Hotel on Longboat Key, and the El Vernona, Ringling's other hotel. He was creating a program for prosperity that was simultaneously a beautification project, grounded in a vision of Sarasota as cultural center for the South.

Among his Sarasota activities, the focus of most public attention was his magnificent Venetian Gothic residence, also nearing completion. Ringling's architect for Cà d'Zan, as he named it, was Dwight James Baum, a prominent New York architect known for his residential work. Baum also designed a number of other buildings in Sarasota, including Ringling's El Vernona Hotel, the county courthouse, the Y.W.C.A. and a Presbyterian church. Many of these were designed in an Italian or Spanish Revival style, inspired by the Mediterranean climate. Simultaneously appearing on Florida's Atlantic coast in Addison Mizner's designs for Palm Beach and Boca Raton, these Mediterranean-style buildings embodied the optimism and exuberance of the Florida boom. Baum was hailed as a standard-bearer of this new regional architectural style, and he was featured internationally in architecture and lifestyle magazines.[4] And Ringling, as the sponsor of so many of these projects, stood poised to make Sarasota the main attraction of Florida's West Coast.

For those who were looking, there was evidence that Ringling had decided to manifest his high standing in the community through the creation of a major art collection. In the spring of 1926, Ringling purchased a series of art objects that were to become some of the most distinctive elements of the future museum building. First he acquired numerous paintings, decorative arts objects, and, most distinctively, the architectural features of entire rooms from the sales of the Astor mansion in New York. Then, through his adviser, renowned art dealer Julius Böhler, he bought the four enormous Rubens cartoons. Commissioned by the Archduchess Isabella Clara Eugenia, these large-scale works had become part of the renowned Duke of Westminster's collection. These purchases indicate that Ringling was already envisioning an art collection on a grand scale. There was no place to put these tapestry cartoons or the Astor items in Ringling's house or, for that matter, in a small museum. Ringling was planning a showplace unlike any other in the United States, with rooms specially designed to display specific works.[5]

Like many of his other purchases from prominent collections, the acquisitions from the Astor sale afforded Ringling much more than fine paintings and elegant decor for his museum.

The dissolution of the Astors' famed double mansion, designed by society architect Richard Morris Hunt, was well-chronicled in the New York papers. Articles recapped the history of the Fifth Avenue palace, providing detailed descriptions of the contents of the rooms, the dresses that Mrs. Astor had worn for particular parties and the guest lists. Press relating to the sale was guaranteed, and Ringling made top billing: "John Ringling Purchases Many Paintings From the Fifth Avenue Mansion."[6] As one of the "heaviest" buyers, Ringling paid some of the highest prices in the auction, including the high price of the entire sale ($10,200) for two Brussels tapestries. He bought the oak paneling and ceiling painting from the library and the gilded paneling from the southwest salon. (For more on these rooms, see the essay by Michael Conforti in this volume.) Special mention was made of his acquisition of Emile van Marcke's *Dans les Landes*, an enormous painting that had occupied a "conspicuous place in the Astor picture gallery and ballroom."

In acquiring such items from the Astor mansion, Ringling was also gaining the social cachet connected with objects from the seat of society's "golden age." For to be "bidden" to an Astor party was to "receive the accolade of society," according to one article. The Astor mansion was touted as "a home in the most luxurious sense of the word... built primarily for entertaining and... the scene of many of the most brilliant functions ever given in New York, including dinners for Prince Henry of Prussia and Prince Louis of Battenberg."[7] As was the case for many other nouveau-riche collectors of the era, the pedigree of the collection afforded Ringling greater respectability. The purchases at the Astor sale and the subsequent acquisition of the Rubens cartoons initiated for Ringling an intense period of collecting across Europe and the United States. The dissolution of significant, historic European collections in the late 1920s represented an unparalleled opportunity for Ringling to acquire an important selection of masters in a short period of time.[8] Many of these sales were carefully covered by the press. While few failed to note the prominent purchases by John Ringling, the press was largely silent on Ringling's plans.

In 1927, at a New York auction of paintings from the well-known collection of Charles Stillman, Ringling acquired Rembrandt's painting, *St. John the Evangelist*. He paid an astonishing $78,000 for the painting — a price overshadowed only by the astronomical $270,000 paid by the

Figure 15. Cypro-Archaic male head, circa 560-450 B.C. Limestone, 12 1/16 x 9 1/4 x 5 inches.

dealer Joseph Duveen for *Titus in an Armchair*, the other Rembrandt in the sale. Prior to the Stillman sale, the highest price paid at an American auction had been $137,000. Ringling bought a total of three paintings at the sale, which was "considered by connoisseurs as an important event in the history of art distribution in this country."[9]

It was not, however, until the 1928 auction of the Metropolitan's Cypriote collection that the establishment of Ringling's Museum came to the attention of the nation's news organizations (fig. 15). Most of the stories generated were based on news from the auction, bolstered by a small handful of interviews that Ringling gave.[10] *Art News*, which had already given much preview coverage to the Cypriote sale, predictably became the first of the art journals to deliver the story. Their front page article explored the mystery surrounding the collection's establishment, explaining that "speculation has led to rumor and rumor has conjured up fantastic visions." With more complete information than any other sources at the time, *Art News* set out to elucidate the record. The article described the holdings of the museum, the handsome architectural setting for the art works, and the proposed advisory structure of the institution. It even delved into the compatibility of Ringling's dual interests — the circus and art worlds.

> *The number of men who are active both as heads of art museums and of circuses is somewhat limited. There are scholarly gentlemen whose candles tremble as the calliope roars past, who may contend that a great chasm exists between the two fields. Pitfalls there may be but there are also many points of contact and the gift of showmanship, the energy, the vitality, the enthusiasm which has made the circus thrilling are excellent qualifications for the man who would meet the old masters on familiar terms.[11]*

In fact, this view seems to reflect Ringling's own perception of himself. He remained, throughout his life, devoted to the Circus, traveling with it virtually every season. No conflict between his pursuits existed in his eyes, and his decades-long dedication to elevating the Circus fits with his efforts to dignify and memorialize his family in the established manner.

The *Christian Science Monitor*, one of the few publications to interview Ringling, also elicited from him some thoughts on the connections between art and the circus. In describing the art of the circus posters, Ringling explained that often "the action of a galloping horse, ... the grace and spirit of a lion at bay, the Hogarthian line of beauty in the pose of a feminine gymnast" were missing. Ringling found this needed vitality in painting.[12] Although this connection has been dismissed as a facile explanation for his collecting tastes,[13] Ringling's unfashionable interest in large-scale Baroque art was not without a sympathetic relation to the aesthetics of the circus, especially as regards the tenor of the 1920s. The compositional dynamism, the extremes of emotion and the colorful palette epitomized by Baroque art all seem most evocative of the circus' rich drama and pageantry. The *Christian Science Monitor* article was reproduced in its entirety in the Sarasota newspaper, a trophy of the national attention that Ringling was bringing to the town.

With perceptions of Ringling colored primarily by his ties to the circus, not all of the coverage was as optimistic or reflective. *The New York Times'* coverage of a sale held by the Metropolitan Museum of Art, at which Ringling purchased Hans Makart's *Diana's Hunting Party*, was typical. While the paper acknowledged the existence of the Sarasota museum, the emphasis remained on Ringling as a circus man whose tastes ran to billboard-size proportions: "Ringling is High Bidder; Circus Man Buys Big Canvas for His Florida Collection."[14] Because of the imprimatur of the collection's originator, the museum was a curiosity to much more than just the art world. The story of Ringling's rise to fame as the circus clown turned financial ringmaster, and — by the time the museum was complete — owner of the largest circus conglomerate in America's history continued to dominate public perception of the man. *The New York World* headline, "Circus King Turns to World of Art," captured the essence of Ringling's attraction for many. While on the one hand Ringling was a cosmopolitan collector, on the other he was characterized as the man "who used to drive a circus wagon." Highlighting the ironic juxtaposition of highbrow and lowbrow, art and circus, one article evoked him as "John Ringing, tall, with the chest of a sea elephant, the chin of a prize fighter, and sensitive, artistic hands."[15]

Some important Ringling purchases evaded this flippant criticism. Ringling's acquisition in 1930 of another large canvas, Peter Paul Rubens' well-known painting, *Pausias and Glycera*, received widespread, enthusiastic coverage (fig. 16). Thought to be a self-portrait of Rubens and his wife in the guise of these characters, the painting had until a few years earlier been in the vast Westminster collection in London, the same collection from which Ringling had earlier bought the enormous Rubens cartoons. Over the years, he acquired several other paintings from this collection as well. *Pausias and Glycera* had been often published in reference works on the master, and had also been included in several public exhibitions. Its purchase was a major coup for Ringling, whose collection was already clearly defined by the Rubens tapestry cartoons acquired some four years earlier. Its popularity with the press was underlined by the oft repeated headline: "Ringling Buys a Rubens."[16]

In general, the paucity of formal interviews with John Ringling, the remoteness of Sarasota and the rumors of the purchase of great numbers of paintings by Rubens and Titian led to much conjecture on the part of some newspapers and art journals. Indicative of the curiosity engendered was a *New York World* article, praising the museum as one of the world's finest: "The galleries in Paris, Florence, London, Dresden, New York, Leningrad and other long famous may have more works of art, but they have none which are finer.... Here is the greatest collection on earth of the work of Peter Paul Rubens.... Here are half a dozen Titians and as many Veroneses."[17] Predictably, this great swell of anticipation and bravura led to some reassessment and retrenching once the museum was finally opened to the public. Although the collection contained some superb masterpieces, it also contained some questionable attributions. Most of all, however, it revealed the personal style of the man who had amassed the collection.

Ringling made an effort to surround himself with recognized and accomplished figures. He retained Julius Böhler, the prominent Munich art dealer who had advised him on much of the collection, as curator for the museum. Ringling also selected a board of directors. He announced the appointment of this roster of distinguished international scholars, dealers, and patrons in the 1928 article in *Art News*, though there is no record of any official action taken by the new board. At the very least, some of these men had intimate access to the works of art. Their interest resulted in further scholarship on the collection, and also more publicity for Ringling. A visit to the Ringling mansion in February of 1927 by Detlev Baron von Hadeln, an authority on Italian art who was one of those named as director in 1928, was chronicled in the *Sarasota Herald*. Von Hadeln proclaimed to the local paper that the museum would make Sarasota one of the art centers of the world. He also issued news of Ringling's plan to establish a school in association with the museum.[18]

Soon after the visit, von Hadeln wrote an article in *The Burlington Magazine* on Ringling's recent acquisition of two allegorical figures by Francesco Guardi. These were, he wrote, outstanding paintings for the new museum then underway. Published in May 1927, the article was probably one of the earliest national mentions of the Ringling Museum. Later that year, in *Art in America*, von Hadeln concluded an article on Paolo Veronese portraits by heralding the large-scale *Portrait of a Family*, in Ringling's collection (pl. 6). Von Hadeln praised the painting as "one of the most important Italian sixteenth century portraits," a stylistic link between Titian and Van Dyck. He deemed it an example of the height of Veronese's portrait painting; the work is, however, today attributed to Giovanni Antonio Fasolo, a student of Veronese.[19] In early 1928, von Hadeln published another article, this one on Ringling's Tintoretto painting, *Samson and Delilah*. He lauded Ringling's version of the painting over the one in the collection at Chatsworth. Von Hadeln called the Ringling painting "in many respects superior to the Chatsworth composition.... It exhibits the full mastery of

The ART DIGEST
Combined with THE ARGUS *of San Francisco*

THE NEWS-MAGAZINE OF ART

A Compendium of ART NEWS *and* OPINION

"Pausias and Glycera," by Peter Paul Rubens and Velvet Brueghel. Purchased by John Ringling for the John and Mabel Ringling Museum. See article on page 8.

Figure 16. Cover of *The Art Digest* magazine, November 1, 1930, with Peter Paul Rubens' *Pausias and Glycera*, purchased by John Ringling in 1930. See Plate 6 for a color reproduction of this painting.

Tintoretto's pictorial craft. The painting of the larger example at Chatsworth is by contrast somewhat dull, and suggests the collaboration of assistants."[20] Von Hadeln's praise of Ringling's collection, and also that of August L. Mayer, another of the appointed directors, seem somewhat effusive, their comments cast primarily in a comparative vein. It seems possible that these men hoped to parlay their relations with Ringling into positions with the fledgling museum. Mayer highlighted an unknown Ribera painting in the Ringling collection, stating that it was more expressive of the artist's workmanship than most of his later Baroque works. He concluded that there were no other Madonnas superior in Ribera's oeuvre, none "so powerful nor so charming as this new acquisition to the most remarkable young gallery of importance in the United States."[21] These articles, written by recognized scholars, brought a measure of certification to Ringling's collecting, a more concrete accolade even than the notable provenances of many of the paintings.

Perhaps more than anything else, it was the building of his museum that garnered sustained attention from the art and architecture communities. John H. Phillips had been engaged as architect by Ringling in 1925, at the very beginning of his collecting effort. The architect was in fact already drafting plans for the building when Ringling informed Böhler of his intentions.[22] Ringling's early commitment to an architect for the museum is evidence of his awareness of architectural symbolism. In an early explanation of his conception of the museum, given to the *Christian Science Monitor* in 1928, Ringling explained:

> *Well, you know from time to time I have found some fifteenth century doors and pillars I liked, I have bought them. The doors are bronze, three pairs of them. The museum garden has an arcade, and some columns I found too, will go there; they belonged once to beautiful Italian renaissance structures. I had to have a permanent place to put those things; I was wanting to build a beautiful memorial. It seemed to me it was time, and what better place could the doors and pillars have?[23]*

The importance architectural style played in Ringling's decisions is evident in his and Mable's flamboyant Venetian Gothic residence, and in the purchase of the Astor rooms for the museum.

Phillips' conception for the John and Mable Ringling Museum of Art produced what was considered to be "one of the most beautiful edifices of its kind in the country."[24] The cloistered courtyard, with one end open to Sarasota Bay, was a breathtaking centerpiece for the museum, and most images of the museum reproduced in magazines featured a view of it. Much was made of this effective amalgamation of "medieval architecture in a modern museum."[25] Variations on the headline "Ringling Art Now in Home Which Is Museum of Architecture"[26] were common.

Art and architecture magazines were filled during the late 1920s with articles featuring the opening of new art museums. By the early 1930s, over 1,000 art museums were operating in the United States, according to the American Federation of Arts.[27] Between 1928 and 1930, museums were opening at the rate of one every two weeks.[28] Many of the articles describing these new museums or installations were authored by men with important ties to the institution, either as director, president or secretary of the board. Ringling did not write any articles, nor did Julius Böhler in his capacity as curator. Böhler labored over a catalogue of the collection, but it was never completed or published. Throughout the period of time in which the museum operated under Ringling's aegis, the only publication that was issued was the *Bulletin of the Ringling School of Art* (ca. 1931).[29] Museum officials around 1930 were defining a new era of professionalism in the field; these articles highlighting their own collections and buildings were in essence a dialogue among colleagues. It is curious that Ringling, whose devotion to the Circus was inextricably linked to the promotional, marketing ethos of that profession, was so silent in the matter of publicizing his own museum. The lack of archival material dating to this period makes analysis difficult. Ringling biographer David Weeks indicates that a local newspaper person served as a publicity relations person.[30] It seems likely from the similar language used in a number of the one-page magazine articles and photo spreads on the new Ringling Museum that a press release was issued, but few indepth profiles of the museum — like those typically found in art journals of the time — were generated.

In addition to features on the establishment of new museums, art journals, like *The Art Digest*, and architectural magazines, such as *Architectural Forum*, frequently addressed the issue of what a building to house an art museum should be like. Technical issues like lighting, temperature control, visitor circulation patterns and the need to combat "museum fatigue" gained currency. Most interesting, however, was the growing trend during the 1920s and early 1930s towards incorporating antique building elements within a museum. The trend existed not only in America, as evinced by the creation in 1930 of the Pergamon Museum in Berlin. Filled with examples of architecture from antiquity, and centered around the recreation of the Pergamon altar, this Berlin museum was hailed as the first purely architectural museum in the world. Perhaps the greatest American example of this movement to incorporate antique elements into modern buildings was The Cloisters.

A unique assemblage of medieval objects, sculpture, and architectural elements collected and exhibited by sculptor George Grey Barnard, The Cloisters had been acquired by the Metropolitan Museum of Art with funds from John D. Rockefeller, Jr. in 1925. Its name derived from the fact that the plan centered around elements from the cloisters of five French monasteries, dating from the twelfth to the fifteenth centuries. Five years later, the Met undertook the construction of a new building on land also donated by Rockefeller at Fort Tryon Park. Completed in 1938, The Cloisters was not a copy of any single building from the Middle Ages, but rather a distinctive twentieth-century structure, planned around the incorporation of numerous, and often large, antique elements.

As profiled in the various journals of the time, this trend manifested itself both in the incorporation of antique (usually medieval) architectural features and in the installation of period (typically Colonial) rooms. Boston, Brooklyn, Minneapolis, and the Metropolitan all featured period rooms. In the new Detroit Institute of Arts, under construction in 1925, architect Paul Cret sought to create a harmonious architectural setting for the objects. One of the museum's highlights was a fifteenth century French Gothic chapel. An important element of the Gothic Hall, the chapel also jutted picturesquely into an outdoor courtyard. Elsewhere in the museum, the gallery with eighteenth century French decorative arts had original panelling, and the Early American hall was housed in a room from the Colonial mansion, Whitby Hall. The Baltimore Museum of Art, scheduled to open in its new John Russell Pope building in 1929, also featured a series of Colonial period rooms.

The new Philadelphia Museum of Art, a Greek temple opened in 1928 atop a hill overlooking the city, was at the forefront of design in its use of period rooms. *American Magazine of Art* wrote that the main exhibition floor was to be a Main Street of design, showing the "pageant of the history of art" through authentic period rooms. When the Gothic and Romanesque sections were opened in 1931, they received extensive press. *Art Digest* explained that the "rooms are not simply four blank walls looking down upon cases and pedestals, but authentic original architectural elements or wall settings, symbolizing architecturally the same spirit and form as the furnishings, tapestries, sculptures and paintings which they enshrine."[31]

This new trend in design grew out of a philosophy articulated by the artist-sculptor-collector George Grey Barnard, the original collector of The Cloisters and also the antiquarian from whom Philadelphia purchased many of their medieval architectural elements. The evocative architectural arrangement that Barnard designed to house the initial Cloisters collection, before it was purchased by Rockefeller for the Metropolitan, inspired the string of what Elizabeth Bradford Smith calls "integrated period settings" for collections in museums around the country. As Philadelphia Museum Director Fiske Kimball articulated it:

> But suppose in this country, where there are no old Gothic churches for our public to pass daily, and where there is no Hotel Cluny to house our collections, we install the objects, uprooted, in neutral halls and galleries. What conception does the great public derive from them of their character as living embodiments in plastic form of the mighty organism of the Middle Ages, with its piety, its chivalry, and its romance? Clearly, architecture itself must here be called into the collections of the Museum — and, if it is not to violate every canon which governs them otherwise — the elements of architecture, like other works displayed, must be original and authentic, not copied.[32]

Ringling's museum was the apogee of such design. Its unique cloistered courtyard evoked an Italian villa and capitalized on Sarasota's semi-tropical setting. Not only did the exterior reflect a sympathy with Renaissance style and atmosphere, but the interior as well created an environs specially suited to the works of art. The Italian gallery (Gallery 3) featured a beamed ceiling and wainscotting from the Villa Palmieri — where Boccaccio was said to have composed the *Decameron*. The entrance to each gallery was flanked by antique columns, or elaborate wooden door surrounds, or mosaic stone surrounds, all of which also had been collected by Ringling. The galleries led directly from one to another, the type of layout that was criticized by some in the museum field as contributing to "museum fatigue."[33] In the Ringling Museum, however, this arrangement created a vista of fanciful and inviting doorways. The *New York Times* featured these allées of ornate door openings in a full-page photo spread on the Ringling Museum: "Antique Doorways Which Complete a Vista: A View Across the Galleries."[34] As virtually the only interior shots featured, these photos would have dominated the reader's first impressions of the museum. The grandest of all the interior spaces was the Rubens gallery, an enormous room with clerestory lighting specially designed to exhibit the cartoons. The door surrounds in this gallery consisted of giant Solomonic columns, echoing those in the cartoons themselves. A stage set for the art, this gallery expressed all of the ideals of the museum.

The building was shown to its best advantage during the official ceremonies marking the dedication of the museum and the concurrent opening of the Ringling School of Art in October 1931. Phillips was in attendance, and remarked on the use of the courtyard as an amphitheatre, much as he had hoped and envisioned.[35] Two thousand people filled the loggias around the terraced gardens to watch the ceremonies. A senator and congressman were there to thank Ringling on behalf of a grateful Florida, and a bishop of the Southern Methodist Church gave a blessing. Interest was not limited to Florida alone. National business and news weeklies covered the activities in Sarasota. TIME in fact seems to have commissioned a second cover portrait of Ringling, by Joseph Margulies (fig. 17), to commemorate what they called "Ringling Day," although the magazine ultimately chose to put the Japanese foreign minister on the cover instead. It seems possible that the editors opted not to use the Ringling cover because at some point during the development of the article, their perspective on the Sarasota story changed; the final publication seems considerably tongue in cheek. Drawing a portrait of Ringling as a Hearstian figure, and the museum as almost a folly, the TIME article began, "There are a Ringling Boulevard and a Main Ringling Boulevard, Ringling Causeway, Ringling Island and Ringling Trust & Savings Bank, but the town is still called Sarasota, Fla."[36] The article then devoted nearly half of its column inches to the history of the Ringling circus endeavor; its references to the art collection dwelled on "mountainous bronze reproductions" and the notion that "Mr. John is still enough of a circus man to like his pictures big." Linked to Florida as the playground of the 1920s and Ringling as the circus dealer, the museum in this depiction seems consigned to a past era.

And in fact, while the opening itself was a positive event for Ringling and a triumphant recognition of his labors for Sarasota, the museum after this time faltered, overshadowed by events in Ringling's personal life. By the end of 1931, financial troubles had virtually brought Ringling's collecting to a halt. The grim realities of his financial picture had already impinged on the full execution of the museum according to original plans. Most especially, the lack of funds had compromised the creation of a complementary school of art, the crux of John and Mable's vision for Sarasota. Ringling's troubled finances, which had previously always been surrounded by a mysterious and wondrous aura of limitlessness, made headlines much more frequently than news of his art ambitions did.

Figure 17. Portrait of John Ringling by Joseph Margulies, circa 1930. Charcoal, opaque white on paper 18 15/16 x 12 3/16 inches. Credit: National Portrait Gallery, Smithsonian Institution.

Ringling's intimate relationships and his health, too, had become front-page material. When Ringling married Emily Buck toward the end of 1930, he was identified in the *New York Times* as the head of the Ringling Brothers-Barnum & Bailey Combined Circus, and only tangentially — at the conclusion of the column — as the owner of "one of the show places of the South [which] houses a notable art collection."[37] The description of the Ringling Museum as a "showplace" can be seen as another example of the press' tendency to view Ringling's endeavors through the lens of the circus. Using the language of the circus, the press paints a picture of Ringling as a showman first of all. Ringling's marriage to Emily Buck lasted only a short while before troubles began, elicited by among other reasons, conflicts over money. Newspapers seemed to exult in the Ringlings' troubles, creating memorable headlines: "Wife Testifies that Life with John Ringling Wasn't Any Circus," and "Ringlings Stage Two Ring Legal Show." The headline "Life Becomes a Three Ring Legal Suit for John Ringling" referred to the other suits pending in addition to the divorce suit Ringling had brought against his wife. Among these numerous lawsuits was one related to questions over the location of Ringling's legal residence. Another concerned the Hotel El Vernona in Sarasota, and yet another was filed by a former oil development partner of Ringling's who claimed to have been induced into signing away oil rights amounting to $10,000.[38]

Few of the newspaper accounts neglected to mention Ringling's deteriorating health. The *New York Times*, in discussing the divorce suit, noted that Ringling's illness had prevented him from touring with the Circus in 1933 for the first time in nearly twenty years.[39] Another story of Ringling's courtroom battles recounted to readers that a nurse was needed to accompany Ringling to the witness stand. One of the more sensational New York papers ran a caption under pictures of the Ringlings stating that "though doctors ordered quiet for [Ringling], [Mrs. Ringling] threw telephone books and pillows during a stormy conference."[40] Various illnesses plagued Ringling the last years of his life. Rumors of his sickness, however, were often much exaggerated. In 1932, Ringling was forced to receive the press in person, in response to stories circulated by the local papers of an infection that had necessitated the amputation of both his legs. Seated in a chair, he swung his legs at the press corps, asking, "Does this look as though either of my legs had been amputated?"[41]

Ultimately, the enduring quality of key aspects of the collection coupled with the unique architectural setting for these paintings helped to elevate the Museum above Ringling's personal troubles. In 1932, the museum was one of eight art museums in the United States featured in *Architectural Forum.* John Phillips' conception for the Ringling Museum was showcased alongside such other masterpieces as the new Baltimore Museum of Art, the Dayton Art Institute, and Paul Cret's design for the Rodin Museum in Philadelphia. These museums, all in grand new edifices, received large photo spreads in the journal.[42] Art historical journals also continued to include essays on works in the Museum. One article discussed the recently re-discovered portrait by Frans Hals of Pieter Jacobsz. Olycan in Ringling's collection, praising the painting as "among the most imposing and impressive of the master's works of the period about 1640, when the artist, who was now fifty-five years old, was begining to give his figures a more monumental aspect."[43] Published in 1935, just over a year before Ringling's death, the article reflected the lasting value of the principal elements of the collection.

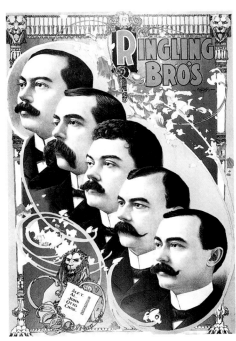

Figure 18. Ringling Brothers poster, 1898, showing, from top: Alf. T., Al., John, Otto and Charles Ringling.

Ringling's driving vision and intense involvement in the establishment of the museum substantively defined the unique nature of the institution. It set the museum apart from other such bequests, which, more typically, were personal collections that became public museums after the donor's death. The absence of museum professionals, a board of directors, or membership in organizations such as the American Association of Museums meant that the Ringling Museum in its first years received little attention beyond notice of the opening. The *Museum News*, the official publication of the American Association of Museums, observed the opening of the Ringling Museum in a short paragraph, adding that Julius Böhler was curator.[44] Other museums emerging during this time typically received more substantial press in the journal's pages, along with an occasional photograph or plan. *The Museum News'* next mention of the Ringling Museum was not until five years later, in Ringling's obituary notice.[45]

Obituaries for John Ringling appeared in all manner of publications, from art magazines to newspapers and news magazines. Above all, they lamented the passing of John Ringling the last of the Ringling Brothers. The "five brothers of Baraboo," as they were called (fig. 18), had "established the ancient pastime of Rome on a scale of American bigness, extravagance and mechanical perfection that attracted capacity audiences even in times of depression."[46] While John Ringling's connection to the public was much stronger as a circus man, he nevertheless dedicated many years and much of his resources in realizing his vision of transforming Sarasota into a cultural center. Amassing an outstanding Baroque art collection emblematic of his flamboyant circus aesthetic, and erecting a Mediterranean-inspired art palace symbolic of Florida's golden age, Ringling established himself as a tastemaker in his own arena. He planned the John and Mable Ringling Museum of Art as the showcase of the town he had adopted and as the appropriate tribute to himself and his first wife. Ultimately, his desired legacy came to fulfillment only after the state of Florida opened the museum to the public permanently in 1947. In time, both the press and the public would come to marvel at Ringling's Italianate jewel on Sarasota Bay.

John and Lulu

The Newly Discovered Correspondence

by Eric M. Zafran

John Ringling and the German art dealer Julius Böhler were introduced in 1922 or 1923, and "Lulu" (as Böhler was called) and his wife Regina soon became the good friends of John and Mable Ringling. The knowledgeable Böhler served Ringling as advisor and confidant and, in 1927, became the curator of the newly-established Ringling Museum of Art (fig. 19).[1] The collection it houses is the direct result of their partnership and stands as one of the great achievements in the history of collecting.

Between the years 1925 and 1931, Ringling and Böhler acquired over four hundred paintings and many examples of the decorative arts. Such concentrated and successful efforts are rare. In an essay written in 1948, Böhler related that once Ringling had decided to build a museum, he purchased and studied many books on art and "became very quickly not only enthusiastic but quite a good judge of pictures," so that in some cases he acted independently against the more prudent advice of Böhler.[2] Actual documentation of their working relationship, however, was lacking. Much of the Ringling material in Sarasota had vanished, and, as David Weeks has noted, the Böhler files in Germany had apparently been "lost in the chaos of World War II."[3] Therefore, when out of the blue, a box of hitherto unknown Böhler and Ringling correspondence and related material arrived last year at the Museum Archive from Böhler's grandson, it was as if a new window had opened on the past. The new material does not answer every question one might have about the museum concept or the acquisition process, nor is it complete. But it does reveal a great deal of new information about their association.

The new material begins in 1927, the year Ringling hired the German dealer — already serving as agent and go-between — as curator of his newly chartered Museum. Two distinct phases of the Ringling-Böhler correspondence are discernible. In the first, which lasts until the summer of 1929, the tone reflects the two men's enthusiasm and excitement as works were pursued and acquired and as the shape of the new collection began to emerge. In the second phase, which lasts from the end of 1929 until Ringling's death in 1936, financial difficulties come increasingly to the fore. As the acquisition period is brought to an end by Ringling's personal and financial crises, he and Böhler struggled to open the Museum and tie up loose ends.

Figure 19. Portrait of Julius Böhler by his father-in-law, the painter, Paul Thiem, circa 1910.

Among Böhler's papers are many letters of inquiry about purchases, loans and jobs. These were generally sent directly to Böhler or forwarded to him by Ringling. The range of the works offered to Ringling was extremely wide. Photographs kept by Böhler depict ancient Egyptian sarcophagi and Greek antiquities as well as early Italian panels and German altarpieces. There is even a curious contemporary painting by Henri Rousseau of a tiger in the jungle — now hanging in the National Gallery in London — priced at $24,000.

The most notable loan request came from A. Everett Austin, Director of the Wadsworth Atheneum in Hartford, who wrote in 1929 seeking loans for an exhibition of Baroque paintings. Ironically, Ringling sent the request on to Böhler. Years later, when Austin, having become the Museum's first director, needed expert testimony about the disrepair into which the collection had fallen, he would invite Böhler back to Sarasota.[4]

Certainly the prize job request came from the young Adelyn Breeskin, who was to become a highly regarded art historian and director of the Baltimore Museum of Art. Breeskin, whose mother had seen Ringling's collection as a weekend guest at his Sarasota home, wrote directly to Böhler in Europe, proposing herself as a "possible assistant to carry out your instructions regarding Mr. Ringling's collection." Böhler's secretary informed the eager would-be assistant that he was away and that she should not expect an answer "for some time."[5]

The direct correspondence between Ringling and Böhler begins on March 6, 1927, by which time they had been working together for almost two years. In the first letter Böhler asked his patron for payment of a variety of bills. The multi-page invoice attached to the letter documents the steady expansion of Ringling's collection. Included in it is Böhler's 10% commission on purchases made of a "large still life by Snyders (pl. 10) (£550), Palma Giovanni [sic] *Venus and Cupid* (£30), and *Lucretia* by Giampetrino (£200)." Purchases from 1926 billed in pounds sterling included a Rubens drawing (£60), Rembrandt's *Lady's Portrait* (£7,900), Velasquez's *Donna Mariana of Austria* (£3114,13), David

Teniers' *Le Mariage de Village* (£1189,10), plus "Five Greek vases very large, two Greek tombstones, one Egyptian Bassorelievo, three Graeco-Indian sculptures all bought at Sotheby's (£250)." There was also the commission on a Giovanni Battista Tiepolo and a Bartolomé Esteban Murillo. The charges continued into 1927 with a Paolo Veronese *Portrait Group* (£3000), the Granacci altarpiece and pictures by Benjamin West (£280) and, again, Murillo (£260). A bill from August 12, 1926 documents a Titian bought for 13,200 German marks, plus 10% commission. Most interesting are the charges associated with the four large Rubens cartoons purchased from the Duke of Westminster. These

Figure 20. School of Titian, *Ecce Homo*, sixteenth century. Oil on canvas, 28 3/4 x 23 1/4 inches. Ringling bought this work as a Titian from Prince Lichnowsky through Julius Böhler in 1927.

included freight, forwarding charges from Eaton Hall, transport insurance, expenses for porters, tips, restoration and fire insurance.

Bills from 1925 and 1926 charged in Swiss francs for the freight from Genoa and insurance on two of the earliest Ringling acquisitions, a Fra Bartolomeo and a Rubens. Finally, there were 1926 charges in dollars for Tintoretto's *Portrait of a Senator* ($15,326), two Jacopo Bassanos ($12,000), a large Bernardino Luini altarpiece with the *Madonna and Saints Roche and Sebastian* ($30,000), Alfred Stevens' *"famous Musician"*(pl. 48) ($1,500), Bassano's *Male Portrait* ($715), and a School of Raphael *Three Kings* ($825); in addition there was a large Venetian frame for the *Samson and Delilah* by Tintoretto ($475).[6]

The postscript to Böhler's covering letter is of special significance for its reference to a "catalogue." It indicates that at this early date he and Ringling were already planning a publication to document the collection for the Museum's opening. The matter of the catalogue will come more to the fore in later correspondence, and in fact one of the treasures of the new material is the draft of Böhler's catalogue text.

Other statements of expenses followed. On March 14, there were charges for forwarding a *Holy Family* and a Rubens and for insurance for the great Frans Hals portrait sent from London to

Munich. Bills from April through June of 1927 document both the continuing activity and the wide range of artists and dealers involved: a Sebastiano Mainardi from Duveen ($11,000); Titian's *Ecce Homo* (fig. 20) from Prince Lichnowsky ($15,179.70), Joseph Israels' *Mother and Child* ($400), the famous Lucas Cranach Portrait of *Cardinal Albrecht of Brandenberg as St. Jerome* (pl. 11) ($10,725), three Antoine Pesne portraits (pl. 45) ($4,950), and a *St. Matthew with the Angel* bought for $1,100 as a Caravaggio and later identified as a Orazio Gentileschi and finally as a Nicolas Régnier (pl. 12). From August there is a bill for two Alonso Cano *Saints in Landscape* for 5,500 marks.[7]

By October of 1927, paintings were arriving in New York. Ringling wrote to Böhler asking for details about the shipments for insurance purposes. "Museum progressing rapidly," he added, "expect to be ready to hang pictures later part of December." Böhler cabled back the contents and values of a shipment of several of Ringling's most important purchases (fig. 21, pls. 13, 14 and 15):

> *Paintings arriving New York two big Carracis [sic] value dollar two fivehundred*
> *pordenone one fivehundred maganza two fifty carlo dolci three stop sorry Chapman*
> *did not advise but Day and Meyer can always see details from consular invoice stop*
> *big Rubenses and others leaving Munich this week Munich writing you stop glad to*
> *hear museum progressing when you are ready to hang please cable.*

He added that he is "hurrying all restorations."[8]

Also included in the new material are several receipts from 1927 made out to Böhler's Lucerne Fine Art Co. by his associates at Henry Reinhardt and Son Galleries of New York. These include Bernardino Licinio's *Family Group* ($2,520), Cranach's *Cardinal Albrecht* ($10,725), and Sir Henry Raeburn's *Elizabeth and Georgiana Reay* ($21,700). To Ringling, the gallery sent the "pedigree" of the magnificent Paolo Veronese, *Flight into Egypt* (pl. 16).[9]

Another set of statements to Ringling follows in the next year. These included a $300 bill from August L. Mayer for a certificate of authentication for a Murillo and a $22,000 bill for the purchase of the Veronese. Repair and restoration bills were included for Frans Post's *Landscape*,

Tintoretto's *Adam*, Robbia's *St. John*, and for a Francesco Zaganelli da Cotignola which was transferred from wood to canvas and relined. There were also charges for the photography, framing and packing of other works and even for cigarettes for Mrs. Ringling.[10] These documents show the extent to which Ringling entrusted Böhler with overseeing the condition of the collection. It is also fascinating to learn of the certificate of authentication, since in general Ringling followed his own judgment or the dealer's. He and Böhler may have felt less sure in the realm of Spanish art.

Böhler and Ringling were together at Sarasota in late 1928 and early 1929. They sent a joint cable in early January to their mutual friend Albert Keller, the manager of the Ritz Carlton in New York City, asking him to attend the sale of art works from the famous Spitzer collection. He was authorized to bid up to $3,000 on paintings by Boucher and was to pursue works by Heda and Canaletto. *The Young Woman with a Letter* attributed to François Boucher was the sole work acquired.[11]

After Böhler returned to Europe, Ringling wrote him one of his longer letters. In it, he informed the dealer that the new museum building

Figure 21. Peter Paul Rubens and Studio, *Abraham and Melchizedek*, from The Triumph of the Eucharist tapestry series, circa 1625. Oil on canvas, 175 1/4 x 224 3/4 inches.

was finished and summarized his purchases at the 1928 Metropolitan Museum sale. Ringling was interested in an enormous Benjamin Constant that had been withdrawn from the auction and returned to the owner's family. "I think I can get it at my own terms," wrote Ringling.[12] Böhler cabled back: "would buy Constant if cheap."[13] Apparently it was, for Ringling did purchase the *The Emperor Justinian* (which, because of its size and poor condition, is now not exhibited). Böhler also reported that he hoped to meet Ringling at Carlsbad and informed him that there would be a great sale in Berlin at the end of May.[14]

These plans had to change, however, for three cables from Ringling to Böhler — each shorter and sadder than the preceding one — followed. In the first, on May 18, 1929, Ringling cites unspecified "matters" delaying his departure. On June 7, he reveals that Mable is gravely ill:

> =account of mable being very seriously ill it is impossible for me at this time to make
> any plans about going to europe i hope you will not let any delay on my part
> interfere with any of your plans luck to you both = john +

On the following day, this laconic notice went out:

> = mable passed away at eight oclock this morning = john +

That Ringling cabled the Böhlers on the very day of Mable's death is strong evidence of his closeness to them at this time.

Their response to his tragic news is not preserved, but Ringling's reply to them at the Ritz in London makes clear that it touched him: "Dear lulu and regina your wonderful cablegram meant more to me than any of the hundreds of messages I received coming as it did from you my nearest and dearest friends."[15] They now resolved that the museum would open as a memorial to Mable, and Ringling seemed to console his grief by throwing himself into his collecting. Before the end of the month, he cabled Böhler: "Sailing tonight on aquitania stop at christies friday there are some large pictures that I thought might go for cheap."[16]

This was Christie's sale of the Princess Paley collection on June 21, 1929, but in the event Ringling bought nothing.[17] However, a week later at the sale of the Comtesse de Behague collection, he made several purchases, including the "Rembrandt," *Descent from the Cross*, for $7,800 (pl. 17).[18] Böhler was not with him at the time, but the dealer promptly cabled his boss at the Savoy Hotel in London: "Congratulate you this was a glorious day awfully tickled you bought Rembrandt because it really might be one stop."[19]

Ringling remained in London for the major sale of the Earl of Yarborough's collection. There, he indulged in what would be his last major splurge of buying. He cabled Böhler the names and prices of his purchases and ended: "for a little sport i purchase the so called rembrandt old lady for five hundred guineas leaving saturday for hotel meurice paris love to both = ringling +"[20] While Ringling stayed on in London, Böhler arranged for the Rembrandt expert Cornelis Hofstede de Groot to examine the "Deposition" painting from the Comtesse de Behague sale. Hofstede de Groot thought it authentic. The work is now attributed to the studio of Rembrandt, but at the time "everybody tremendously excited am so happy you own now one of Rembrandt's masterpieces stop I was right after all."[21]

This happy moment in the summer of 1929 can now be seen as the apogee of the relationship between Ringling and Böhler. The impending Depression would exact a toll on both their collecting activities and their personal friendship. Thus we pass to the second phase of the Ringling-Böhler correspondence, in which the focus begins to shift from news of exciting acquisitions to more mundane financial matters and in which a marked cooling of affection eventually became perceptible. In September, Ringling's return to Europe was delayed by what he called "the big circus deal"— his attempt to gain control of the rival American Circus Corporation.[22] The stock market crash later in the year would turn this deal into a terrible financial burden from which he would never escape. On September 9, though, Böhler could still cable him in New York to "congratulate you on your big deal am so happy it came through and hope it will be a very big success."[23]

In the same missive Böhler also discusses what, along with the museum catalogue, was to become the chief concern of the remaining years of his work with Ringling. This was the status of two paintings originally acquired as part of the enormous Emile Gavet collection. (The full history of this collection is analyzed by Deborah Krohn in her contribution to this volume.)

The painting in question was a double-sided altar wing — one of the earliest known works by the Swiss master Nicklaus Manuel Deutsch. One side depicted St. Eligius in his goldsmith's workshop and the other, the meeting of Anna and Joachim at the Golden Gate.[24] For some reason, perhaps because this was a significant example of early German-Swiss art that could be reunited with the other existing double sided panel, Ringling was intent on selling or trading this major masterpiece, rather than preserving it in his museum. Their first hope was to trade it for works in the collection of the German Crown Prince. Several trades were discussed through the Prince's agent but came to nothing. Böhler then contacted the Swiss government, which — after protracted negotiations that are tracked in the correspondence — eventually purchased the panel. [25]

Böhler and Ringling continued to exchange information about the auction sales on both sides of the ocean. Ringling attended the 1930 sale of Mrs. H.O. Havemeyer's collection in New York and bought a Goya and a Veronese he had unsuccessfully bid on at the first Holford sale three years earlier. "Glad you bought Goya and Veronese both fine," cabled Böhler.

In May, Ringling cabled that he would "probably be delayed a little bit in sailing this year on account of rather big deal." [26] This was undoubtedly Ringling's purchase for two million dollars of his few remaining circus rivals. [27] Böhler, however, responded with friendly chastisement: "wish you would come all the same business is not everything health ought to come first and you need the cure." [28]

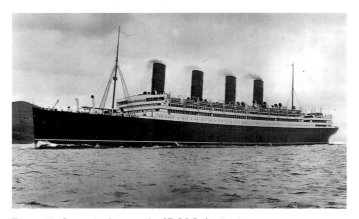

Figure 22. Souvenir photograph of R.M.S. Aquitania. Photograph: Corbis - Bettmann.

Ringling crossed over to Europe, hoping to meet Böhler in Paris. As it turned out, the two men were not able to get together before Ringling had to sail back on the R.M.S. Aquitania in July.[29] After his return to America, Ringling focused on the catalogue and the Museum. He had opened the art galleries to the public for one day at the end of March, but he needed a catalogue of the collection for a proper formal opening. Having finally received the photographs taken by V. Sakayan, Böhler reported that most of them were not of satisfactory quality for reproduction. According to Ringling, the request that they be reshot caused the touchy photographer to threaten a lawsuit.[30] Despite this difficulty, Ringling was eager to open the museum in January of 1931. By this time, Böhler candidly doubted a catalogue of adequate quality could be completed by then. To Ringling's request that he come to Sarasota in November, Böhler countered with an early January departure date and proposed a "provisional finely illustrated catalogue."[31] Unhappy, Ringling cabled: "terribly disappointed as i figured we could have catalogue and everything ready to open in january."[32]

After New Year's, Ringling — who had in the interim married Emily Haag Buck — was even more insistent: "Please send at once any material for catalogue so can get this started immediately."[33] Böhler responded with a long letter. After congratulating Ringling again on his new marriage, Böhler cited three reasons for his and Regina's delay in leaving Europe. First, business had been poor, and his father had opposed his going to the States, where business seemed likely to be even poorer. Second, he and Regina were building a new house and had been engrossed in construction details. Finally, he had been trying to close the sale of the Deutsch panel to the Swiss government.

Böhler then broached the issue of the catalogue: "Now comes the most ticklish question of all and one in which I am afraid you do not agree with me. You know I mean the catalogue." The dealer had by this time realized that rushing a poor catalogue into publication would not help the museum but would certainly damage his own credibility. He asked Ringling to be patient, arguing that "if we want to make a scientific catalogue we must take the time necessary for it." Böhler had consulted the experts about publication times, and the news was not good. New catalogues by Friedländer and Hermann Voss in Berlin "took an average of three to four years."

Böhler went on to say that Voss, who was lecturing at the Art Institute of Chicago in March, promised to meet him in Sarasota to look at the collection, and he asked Ringling to pay his fare and show him hospitality. Since the catalogue would not be ready for the museum opening, Böhler proposed two temporary publications in its stead: a short catalogue, without reproductions, listing the collection's holdings and a second publication consisting only of reproductions of 75 of Ringling's paintings. "Please, John," wrote Böhler, "let me have my way in this."[34]

Ringling did not really like the idea of the reduced catalogue, and there was a last minute rush to produce the larger version. The poor quality of many of the photographs, however, was again the sticking point. Cables went back and forth, Ringling prodding and Böhler pleading, but the catalogue wasn't coming together. Ringling was forced to push the date of the formal opening back into February as he waited impatiently for Böhler's arrival in Sarasota.

Böhler, however, finally had to admit that he would not be at the opening: "Hear you open Museum this week heartiest congratulations sure it will be great success stop cannot get away. . . am terribly disappointed."[35] Ringling responded that he too was "terribly disappointed you can't come no date set for opening however. Will open in about two weeks without catalogue will advise dates later."[36] As it turned out, Ringling opened the Museum for just a week in March. It did not formally open to the public until nearly a year later, on January 17, 1932.[37]

More anxious cables and nightletters were exchanged before Böhler's compromise catalogue finally arrived in Sarasota. The catalogue Ringling received is lost, but the new trove of material includes various lists of the collection and several stages of catalogue drafts. The number of entries varies from 182 to 336, and what appears to be a final draft lists 281 works. Although these are not arranged in alphabetical or chronological order, one list is broken down by schools and shows a logical division of the works into Early Italian, Late Italian, German and Flemish Primitives, Flemish, Dutch, English, French, Spanish, and Modern. The last category, the most unexpected, consists primarily of nineteenth century works by Alfred Stevens, Joseph Israels, Ferdinand Roybet, Constant Troyon, Rosa Bonheur, and a little known American artist Carl von Marr.

The format of the catalogue was to provide for each painting a rather chatty artist's biography, a description of the work and subject depicted, references to publications and an abbreviated provenance. The latter included neither auctions nor the dealers — such as Böhler himself — who had acted as intermediaries in supplying works to Ringling. Also lacking was the discussion of attribution and dating that has become standard in modern collections catalogues. Still, it was for the time an extremely detailed and serious undertaking. If published, it would have been a model of its kind far in advance of most other American museums.

Meanwhile, negotiations over the Deutsch panel were continuing. Böhler now had an offer of 300,000 francs from the Swiss government.[38] He invited Ringling to vacation with him in Carlsbad in the summer: "I am sure it is going to do you a lot of good." Ringling cabled back that he expected to sail in June and "could go directly to Carlsbad."[39] By then, however, Böhler had to change his plans and was too busy to holiday in Carlsbad.[40] The two tried to meet in Berlin, Paris, and London, but oddly could never connect. Finally, on July 7, Böhler wrote to Ringling in London that he "hopes you will have a good crossing and to see you in Sarasota beginning November."[41]

The attempted sale of the Deutsch panel dominates the correspondence for the rest of 1931. By this time, the Swiss had lowered their offer to 200,000 francs. Böhler nevertheless urged Ringling to take it. Ringling, having hoped to get 300,000 or at least 250,000 francs, was at first unwilling to accept. But he grudgingly gave in to Böhler's advice — on the condition that the Swiss would "close the deal immediately."[42] That was not possible, Böhler cabled back, since the purchase still depended on a vote of approval by the Swiss government.[43] Ringling then got anxious and sent Böhler a cable asking for their payment.[44] He followed this with another a few days later, since he was eager to know their answer "for financial reasons."[45] Böhler's reply could not have pleased him: on "account of times Bern people have difficulties" and would not make a decision until November. For the same reason, Böhler continued, he himself would not come over in the fall.[46]

Figure 23. Photograph of Julius Böhler, circa 1950.

Meanwhile the global financial crisis continued to worsen. A tone of increasing anxiety and hints of doom creeped more and more into the correspondence. Not only would he be prevented from traveling to Sarasota, Böhler explained in a long letter, but bad times required him to prepare Ringling's account for the previous two years and ask for immediate payment.[47] It was at this time that Ringling's illness first developed.[48]

By March, 1932, Böhler had learned that Ringling was not well and sent a wish for his speedy recovery. He also congratulated Ringling on the new Art School and was pleased to have seen Ringling's three Rembrandts reproduced in the new monograph by Wilhelm Valentiner. But there is also bad news about the Deutsch panel. The Swiss offer was apparently a package combining government and corporate funds. But the financial crisis had forced a Bern corporation to withdraw its commitment, putting the whole offer in jeopardy. Finally, Böhler included his own bill, for the second time: "I need the money quite badly."[49]

Nearly six months went by before Ringling responded with a curt and rather sarcastic cable hinting at his own perilous state: "is there anything from the swiss would come in handy at this time."[50] Böhler's letter dated the following day was not really a direct answer, and he seems to have been unaware of Ringling's serious illness and financial straits. In any case, he could offer no relief, for, as he relayed, the Swiss had dropped their offer to 150,000 francs and then again to 110,000. At that point, Böhler had broken off the negotiations. "I thought it was the only way to deal with these people," he wrote to Ringling, "and I hope you agree with me." Böhler ended with yet another request for payment.[51]

In November of 1933, Ringling, hounded by creditors, had to write to Böhler for an evaluation of the collection:

> *please cable me actual value of my art collections also present sales value stop they are not for sale but want this statement as high a figure as possible to establish my credit love regina and you = ringling +*[52]

Böhler cabled back his estimate of $4 million.[53] Böhler himself was hurt by the Depression, and in his next letter to Ringling he reported that he and Regina were forced to give up their house. On the Deutsch panel, Böhler advises Ringling to let him approach the Swiss with a figure of $35,000. In view of the situation, nothing higher would have been realistic. "Don't take too long," he cautioned Ringling, "because it might get too late."[54]

The correspondence resumes, after another long gap, in July of 1935, when Ringling sent Böhler a final letter. Obviously frustrated, Ringling asks his dealer:

if there are any pictures in my collection which you think you could sell in Europe as
it would be a great advantage to me if I could sell a few hundred thousand worth of
my pictures now and buy examples by the same artists back a little later when I am
all straightened out.[55]

Fortunately for the collection, Böhler did not act on Ringling's request. In what appears to be his last letter to Ringling, he reports on August 1, 1936, that "we instructed our bank to remit to you in Sarasota $28,775 being full payment for the 2 pictures by Nic. Manuel Deutsch. . . . With this payment your debts to us and ours to you are wiped out."[56] On this balanced and rather impersonal note the remarkable saga of the German dealer and the American collector came to an end. Ringling died in December of the same year, but his and Böhler's joint achievement lives on in Sarasota.

In and Out of the Auction House

Collector to Connoisseur

by K. Lee De Groft

> *Rarely does a man arise upon a certain morning and announce abruptly, over his breakfast coffee, 'Today I shall begin a collection!'...For the processes leading up to the birth of a collector are often slow and inconspicuous.* [1]

"Inconspicuous" perfectly describes John Ringling's development as a collector and also his later acquisition style. Ringling's emergence as an aesthete took place over a quarter of a decade. During that time, he studied priced catalogues, analyzed provenance and attributions and established a strong relationship with a reputable and expert dealer. Although essentially self-taught, he followed most of the established rules for aspiring American collectors of the early twentieth century.

Successful American museums that developed during this time were in general formed according to the master plan of a collector or founder. The time span between the conception of the Ringling Museum and its opening was a mere seven years. Yet the quality and character of its collection does not indicate a hasty accumulation. In fact, Ringling set about making himself into a connoisseur long before he revealed his dream of a Sarasota art museum. Once committed to that dream, he brought diligence, strategy and financial resources to bear in order to build the major art collection now associated with his name.

Ringling's interest in the fine and decorative arts goes back to the early years of the twentieth century, when he first began to frequent auctions and estate sales. Research indicates that there was at least one accumulation of artworks predating the Museum collection. Ringling was apparently unsatisfied with the result, however, and sold the lot.[2] The contents and location of this initial effort are unknown. We do know, though, that Ringling bought primarily at auction. The refinement of his taste through the correction of past mistakes can thus to some extent be tracked through early sales catalogues.

Note: The author was assisted by Deborah Walk and Jan Silberstein in the research and production of this essay.

Education through Catalogues

John was not going to undertake [the Museum] without gathering as much
knowledge as possible and actually within a very short time he became quite a good
connoisseur
...books...Catalogues! Museum visits...[3]

One of the first pieces of advice given to would-be collectors is to study auction catalogues. John Ringling certainly followed this suggestion. He conscientiously pored over his vast collection of pamphlets, brochures and catalogues, diligently recording prices and making notes. In this, he fit the classic mold of the collector. One satire from the period humorously observes that the consummate collector spends so much time studying prices and provenance that he loses sight of the art and ends up as a passionate collector of art catalogues.[4]

Ringling received catalogues from the major New York and London auction houses. The bulk are from major auction houses such as the American Art Association and the Anderson Gallery in New York, and Christie's and Sotheby's in London. But small auction houses and several German galleries are also represented. The John Ringling Papers contain over seven hundred auction catalogues from 1866 to 1936. Seventy-one of them bear hand-written markings by Ringling or his wife Mable. Ringling also made a point of requesting and paying for "priced" copies of catalogues. Supplied by the auction houses following major sales, these contained purchase amounts and the names of buyers. When priced catalogues were not available, Ringling created his own. Julius W. Böhler, the German dealer through whom Ringling acquired the bulk of his works, claimed Ringling spent his spare time scrutinizing these sale records and memorizing pertinent details. Anecdotes abound of Ringling's ability to astound other collectors and dealers by reeling off the provenance and prices of works in their possession.

Education through Auction

He goes to auctions of paintings; he sits in corners unnoticed, occasionally he bids,
more often bids are made for him; when the auctions close he is immediately as
completely gone as a forgotten thought, with none to say when or which way he
went.

— *June 19, 1928,* Sarasota Herald, *on John Ringling*[5]

If Ringling used the auction house as a kind of classroom and auction catalogues as his textbooks, he also, like many self-made men of the period, held his cards close to the vest. While some of his high-profile acquisitions — such as his purchases from the 1926 sale of the Astor mansion in New York — were of a flamboyance befitting a circus king, his presence and buying strategies were more frequently subtle and discreet.

Ringling did not reveal his museum plans to Böhler until 1924 or 1925, roughly a year after they first met. By that time, Ringling had been attending auctions for many years. A 1928 interview reported that Ringling had been collecting art for twenty-five years, which would date his first acquisitions to around 1903 when Ringling was in his late 30s. In Mable Burton, whom he married in 1905, Ringling found a mate with whom he could share his growing fascination with art. The newlyweds kept two homes — a summer place in Alpine, New Jersey and an apartment on Fifth Avenue. In 1911 they added the Palms Elysian house in Sarasota.

John and Mable furnished these homes themselves, through purchases at auctions.[6] Most of the offerings in these estate disposals were household items such as lace curtains, hooked rugs and kitchen tiles. The grand houses frequently contained Old Master paintings and other works of fine art, however, and the exposure to art collections at auctions such as the 1916 Davanzati Palace sale in New York seems to have stimulated the Ringlings' interest in and desire for higher works of art.

This sale is of special interest. The Davanzati was a Florentine Renaissance villa and was very similar in style to the Ringling's later residence, Cà d'Zan. From majolica, Italian textiles and iron work to sixteenth and seventeenth century Italian paintings, the Davanzati collection, in many ways, foreshadowed the furnishing of the Ringling's own palace. Serendipitously, a painting Ringling saw at this 1916 sale was one he ultimately purchased almost fifteen years later. The piece, Raffello Gualterotti's, *Giuoco del Calcio—Piazza Santa Croce* or more familiarly referred to as "Football in Florence," was for sale again in 1931, whereupon Ringling promptly bought it. If the stories concerning Ringling's prodigous memory are even partially true, he no doubt recalled the first time he and Mable saw the work years before.

A comparison of catalogues from this period to those after 1924 points to Ringling's growing seriousness and sophistication. The tone of his earlier margin notations is casual and social — they typically indicate which room of which house would receive the object in question, where to ship the piece and even when to get lunch. Around 1921, however, a noticeable shift becomes visible.

The change follows a 1920 sale Ringling attended in New York, at which he may have bought three paintings. Ringling's copy of the catalogue, *Sale of Furnishings and Early American and British Portraits*, contains prices for virtually every item.[7] Compared to the works he later collected for the Museum under Böhler's guidance, those Ringling flagged at this sale seem atypical. Among them were three landscapes by American painter Thomas Doughty, a depiction of the signers of the Declaration of Independence in a set of fifty-four oil portraits and an Audubon bird scene. None of these is in keeping with his later collection.

Several prices in Ringling's copy of the catalogue are circled, possibly indicating that he purchased them. Ringling's typical practice in later years was to record a bidding price next to items which interested him. He then circled those he bought and adjusted the prices when a discrepancy existed. In the catalogue to this 1920 sale, he circled and corrected the prices next to the following three works: John Cole, Jr.'s *Portrait of a Man*, $111; Alvan Fisher's *River Landscape with Horseman*, $65; and John Vanderlyn's *Portrait of a Man*, $60. The purchases cannot be verified as Ringling's, however, since the records from this sale only identify the purchasers of major pieces and do not include those mentioned above.

The quality and even the authenticity of many pieces in the sale were rather severely called into question by *Art News*. The article — censoriously called "Lessons from a Sale" — charged that the works were on the whole inferior in quality and often did not well represent the artists in question. The article advised against relying on supposed experts or agents and exhorted collectors to increase their own knowledge of art and collecting. It closed with a warning to fledgling and would-be American collectors to be wary of collecting "names" without questioning quality.[8] It seems Ringling, a subscriber to *Art News*, took the advice to heart, for soon after the publication of the critical article, his catalogue notations become more skeptical and circumspect. Ringling was maturing as a collector and he even later noted that his own viewpoints and tastes were developing during this early time.

Education through Association

The friendships Ringling formed at this time with other connoisseurs also contributed to his growing sophistication and influenced the direction of his tastes. It has been said that there were few "responsible and competent experts and advisers" to guide and mentor beginning American collectors.[9] Ambitious Americans would have needed to make European connections. Ringling did just that, employing agents in major and lesser galleries. More significantly, he sought out the counsel and friendship of learned men, namely the German dealer Böhler and the private collector Albert Keller.

Böhler's influence on Ringling has been widely noted. (see Eric Zafran's essay on their correspondence in these pages) Keller, however, was the man who first brought Ringling and Böhler together. A business associate of Ringling's and a friend of Böhler's, Keller was then the manager of the Ritz Carlton in New York. As early as 1920, Ringling was considering building another Ritz Carlton in Sarasota. According to Weeks, Ringling brought Keller down to Florida around 1921 to get his input on a location for a hotel (fig. 24). Socially, John and Mable were "frequent guests" at the Keller apartment during 1922 and 1923. Ringling may have acquired some of his new-found interest in Baroque and Old Master paintings from Keller, who owned works by Peter Paul Rubens, Fra

Figure 24. Photograph of (from left) John Ringling, Mable Ringling, two unidentified women and Albert Keller, circa 1925.

Angelico and Rembrandt.[10]

Böhler initially worked through Reinhardt Galleries in New York. Later he followed the practice of many European dealers and established a branch of his own firm in the art-mad city. Along with his partner and brother-in-law Fritz Steinmeyer, Böhler opened an office in Suite 728 of the Ritz Carlton around 1928. Böhler's financial records reveal that Keller worked in some capacity in the acquisition of pieces. A 1927 invoice listed the following three works as "sold to Ringling;" Bernardino Licinio's *Family Group*, Lucas Cranach's *Cardinal Albrecht as St. Hieronymous*, and Sir Henry Raeburn's *Portrait of Elizabeth and Georgiana Raey*. The invoice also says "Albert Keller has as a commission from the Ringling sales, kept a Riccio bronze valued at $550 and a small sculpture by de Vois valued at $300."[11] It is unclear what works comprised this "Ringling sale," but it is quite obvious that Keller had an early and continuing involvement in the acquisition of works for Ringling's collection. In 1929, Keller attended the Spitzer sale in New York and bid on items for Ringling and Böhler. This association between the three men was fairly well known among the auction houses and shipping agents. Also, paintings which arrived in New York in Ringling's absence were routinely sent to Keller at the Ritz Carlton for safe keeping.

Both Keller and Böhler became Ringling's friends as well as business associates, and the men often combined business trips with pleasure. Mable Ringling, Regina Böhler, and Clara Keller, frequently joined their husbands on excursions in America and abroad. The couples traveled the great steamships of the time — the Aquitania, the Bremen, the Leviathan and the Mauretania (fig. 25) — often with newly acquired works of art on board. Ringling named Keller and Böhler to the board of directors of the Art museum in 1928. In addition, Böhler became the museum's first curator. Other museum directors named by Ringling included leading German scholar and curator Max Friedländer, art historian and curator August Mayer, famed British dealer Sir Joseph Duveen and renowned Venetian painting expert Detlev Baron von Hadeln.[12] These positions were merely titular, however, and there is no evidence that the Board of Directors ever met in any official capacity during John Ringling's lifetime.

Aside from Böhler and Keller, none of the other directors played an active a role in the formation of the Museum. But they did occasionally exert influence on Ringling's decisions. Duveen, for example, was the source for several of the finest pieces in the Ringling collection, including Thomas Gainsborough's *Portrait of General Philip Honywood* (the largest known work by the artist) and Joshua Reynolds' *Portrait of the Marquis of Granby* (pl. 18). Ringling and Duveen were businessmen first and foremost, and it is unclear who was cultivating whom. Duveen obviously recognized Ringling as a potentially valuable customer, and for his part Ringling realized that association with the Duveen name would benefit him and the Museum.

Figure 25. The luxury steamer Mauretania, circa 1920s. Photograph: Corbis - Bettmann.

As for Baron von Hadeln, Ringling was familiar with his published works on the Venetian masters and owned several of his books on late Renaissance Italian painting. Ringling apparently sought Hadeln's opinion, for several of Ringling's auction catalogues bear inscriptions noting Hadeln's suggestions. Ringling did not, however, always heed that advice. Next to a catalogue entry for a work by Bellini, Ringling wrote: "Hadeln said to buy it but?"[13] Whatever his reservation concerning the work was, it was sufficient to dissuade him from acquiring it. No longer a mere novice, Ringling was depending more on his own knowledge and intuition.

An American Collector in King Edward's Court

A quiet-looking man at Christie's sale room yesterday caught the eye of the auctioneer, raised his eyebrows, and gave the slightest possible inclination of his head. Suppressed excitement filled the room, which was crowded with art lovers and dealers from all

over the world. The auctioneer's keen glance swept the room as he raised his right

arm and held it poised for a moment in the air. Then the hammer fell. The tension

of the audience ended in a gasp of relief, followed by hearty applause.[14]

The auction houses of the 1920s and 1930s were a uniquely exciting arena. Some of the most important sales took place in England. Indeed, by the 1920s a vast quantity of art from old British collections was moving across the Atlantic. This was due to recent legislation passed by Parliament that allowed distressed British landowners to dispose of their properties and collections, combined with a new exemption in the U.S. on import taxes on art purchases. The unique situation — which collectors such as J.P. Morgan, William Randolph Hearst and George Blumenthal moved quickly to take advantage of — happened to coincide exactly with the high point of Ringling's personal fortune. Wittingly or not, this was the time Ringling began collecting in earnest.

In general the "American collector" was not much esteemed in Great Britain or on the continent. Friedländer in particular decried the American practice of "buying artists' names instead of pictures...and paying substantial sums for certificates of authenticity."[15] The idea prevailed that American collectors were being "swindled" by buying fake paintings with fake certificates. According to one art dealer of the time "Americans have bought within a short period $10 million's worth of pictures whose certifications are indefensible."[16] There is record of only a handful of certificates of authenticity purchased by Ringling. Among them is one from Dr. Hermann Voss, of the Kaiser Friederich Museum in Berlin, confirming a Giovanni Battista Piazzetta.

Frequent articles and even speeches in Parliament lamented the loss of Britain's art treasures to Americans, and vague "anti-Yankee" sentiment is evident in auction accounts from the period. The few times Christie's mentioned Ringling in their season catalogues, it was always as "the Modern Barnum." On each occasion the auctioneers claimed, perhaps rightly, that he delighted in the appellation. The 1931 account of the auction season, however, closes with a more deferential description. "Mr. Ringling also put in a welcome appearance...he is astute enough to have many good pictures to exhibit to the American public," says the auction house.[17] One assumes that the roughly half a million pounds Ringling spent at Christie's by this time accounts for his warm "welcome."

The discomfort with American collectors sometimes displayed by the British and Germans paled, however, before the disdain openly expressed by French connoisseurs. Their general attitude is summed up by international art dealer René Gimpel, who writes in his diary: "I often reproach myself with not having noted down descriptions of American collectors, but I declare I have nothing to say about them, as they have so little personality. They show you all their pictures like rich children showing off their toys."[18] Gimpel wrote this in March of 1929, at the height of the American influx into Europe and Great Britain. As for Gimpel's opinion of Ringling, he mentions him only once in passing as "the one-time clown." Perhaps the continental attitude expressed here is one reason Ringling preferred to limit his purchases of paintings abroad to Great Britain and Germany.

The lack of American interest in Italian art was also noted.[19] After the turn of the century, however, many American collectors — among them Samuel Kress, Henry C. Frick, Isabella Stewart Gardner and Henry Walters — were actively acquiring Italian art. Ringling himself bought works by Jacopo and Giovanni Bellini, Luini, Carpaccio, Giovanni Battista Moroni, and Francesco Guardi. The high point of his Italian acquisitions was certainly the 1927 Holford sale at Christie's in London.

"Virgins, Saints, and Martyrs"

The sale of the Holford Italian paintings was a cultural event in itself. Böhler excitedly wrote Ringling with the news of the impending sale, exclaiming: "It is the Holford collection that is going to be sold! This is very important, a very rare occasion...there are a lot of fine things just for us which ought not to fetch much."[20] The sale represented one of the last great house collections and is still considered by Christie's to be a marker in its history. Some of the prices attained were considered "abnormal," and the total sale realized nearly £156,000. Lorenzo Lotto's *Lucretia* sold for a staggering £23,000 — the highest price attained for a single piece at the sale. Several other works sold for over £10,000. But these high points aside, most of the works were relatively inexpensive.

The potential for bargains did not fail to attract John Ringling. It is still unclear whether he himself attended this first Holford sale, but his and Böhler's buying strategy and use of purchasing agents emerge vividly from their inscriptions on the auction catalogues. In his copy, Ringling marked in pencil the price or price range he was willing to bid. In a different copy Böhler indicated who was to bid on or purchase the piece. The proposed price for each was figured in British pounds, with the U.S. dollar equivalent in parentheses next to it. Five different agents were designated bidders for Böhler and Ringling at this sale: Arthur U. Newton, a picture dealer; the Raeburn Gallery; Alec Martin, an associate with Christie's; Goldschmidt, of the London Goldschmidt Gallery; and an individual identified as E. Böhler, possibly Julius Böhler's son.

In Böhler's copy of the catalogue, these names are written next to the bidding prices. Next to several items are the initials "J.R."; in nearly all of these instances, Böhler himself acted as the official buyer. Ringling obtained the largest number of works at this sale. The marked catalogues indicate that Ringling and Böhler were seeking 51 works — nearly half of the total number offered. Of these, they ultimately obtained 21.

Among "the ones that got away" was the piece Ringling considered to be the "best one." He planned to bid between $2000 and $3000 for *Adoration of the Shepherds* by Bonifazio Di Pitati. Martin was authorized to bid up to £650 ($3200), but it sold to another dealer for £1102 10s — nearly double Ringling's maximum. Other notations in Ringling's catalogue reveal that he was looking quite closely at the works and their attributions. Catalogue entry number 82 consisted of *The Madonna of the Meadow*, attributed to the School of Bonifazio. Ringling indicated next to the catalogue entry "Waagen says by Palma Vecchio." Prepared to pay £200, Ringling lost the piece to Leggatt for £1365.

In most cases the highest dollar prices indicated in Ringling's catalogue correspond exactly to those marked in Böhler's catalogue. But there was one interesting exception. The Holford sale included a *Portrait of the Queen of Cyprus*, attributed to Titian. Ringling indicated a top price of $12,000, the highest amount marked in his catalogue. Böhler believed the work was "cheap" for £4000, or $20,000. Böhler's opinion must have prevailed, for he ultimately paid £4200 for the piece, making it the most expensive acquired by Ringling at the sale.

Ringling had his own opinions of certain pieces and questioned the attribution of a work by an unknown artist, listed only as "Venetian School." Next to this picture, entitled *The Muse of Painting*, he wrote "Veronese," and a price of $1500. Though Böhler was prepared to bid up to that price, the painting went to the London art dealer Thomas Agnew. Ringling's curiosity seemed piqued by this possibly mis-attributed Veronese. He did not, however, express an interest in the *Diana and Acteon* by Veronese. The piece did catch Böhler's eye, and he wrote a note to "buy if possible cheap for £1000." He made a similar notation next to two other Veroneses in the sale, though Ringling had not marked either of them. Each of the three Veroneses sold for well over Böhler's proposed bids for the works.

There was one work in the sale, however, that did later prove to be by Veronese. For a life sized portrait by Girolamo Romanino, Ringling indicated a top price of $10,000 in his catalogue, while Böhler prepared to bid on Ringling's behalf in the range of £1200 ($6000). At some point Böhler noted, "you can go much higher..." The piece went to a dealer named Coureau, who had purchased several Egyptian antiquities on behalf of Ringling the year before. The work reappeared on the market in 1930, whereupon Ringling purchased it as a Veronese. He clearly remembered its earlier attribution when he cabled the news of his purchase to Böhler. "Purchased fifty-five hundred Veronese life sized portrait bearded man with dog which was in first Holford sale as Romanino...," crowed Ringling.[21] Prepared to pay $10,000 three years earlier for the same piece as a Romanino, Ringling got the painting for only slightly more than half that.

The use of agents at auction was, of course, a strategy to conceal Ringling's identity as the real bidder. Böhler's correspondence indicates that by 1928 his relationship with Ringling was no secret. And in any case Ringling announced Böhler's official affiliation with the Museum in that year. But no automatic association existed between Ringling and the dealers Newton, Martin and Goldshmidt. While Martin was associated with Christie's, the others were private dealers. Apparently, they did not add a commission to the auction prices, indicating that Ringling probably paid them a flat rate for their services as bidders. Without doubt, the strategy enabled Ringling to buy works discreetly, and it probably saved him a significant amount of money. Ringling's focus on prices must also be understood as simply an extension of his deal-making personality.

Out of the Auction House

Aside from some noteworthy exceptions, Ringling acquired most of his collection at auction. In a few instances, he located works himself, decided to buy them and then brought Böhler in to act for him. Curiously, some of the most well known pieces in the collection are those Ringling bought on his own.

Among them were the four Rubens tapestry cartoons — the showpieces of the Ringling Museum. Originally a part of the Duke of Westminster's 1922 auction sale, the cartoons had failed to meet their reserve prices.[22] Undeterred by the enormous size of the works, Ringling tracked them down and later directed his architect to design a Museum where they would be the first works to greet the visitor. Though he thought the purchase price too high, Böhler closed the deal on Ringling's behalf.

A certain degree of mystery surrounds Ringling's purchase of the Franz Hals portrait of Pieter Jacobsz. Olycan (pl. 19). Böhler himself recalled that the picture hung in an English country house and was purchased for £20,000. When Dutch expert Cornelis Hofstede de Groot was taken out to the house to authenticate the piece, he was kept ignorant of where he was going or to whom the painting belonged. Soon after, the painting showed up in the possession of A. Reyre, a picture dealer in London. While it was assumed that the painting was somehow acquired by Ringling later, recent research reveals that the Ringling Museum was its destination all along. The Böhler papers indicate the painting was bought from a Major Bretherton, at whose country estate Hofstede de Groot had seen it. Its brief stay at the Reyre Gallery was but one stop on its way to Sarasota, and records show that Ringling paid commissions to Reyre at the time the Hals was purchased. Furthermore, registration records include a photograph of the Pieter Jacobsz. Olycan with a handwritten note from Böhler reading: "This portrait is for sale in England, for me one of the finest portraits by Hals...one of the strongest, and expressing a wonderful type of man." Works by Hals were much sought after at this time. Shortly after Ringling bought the Olycan portrait, Duveen, who had paid £30,000 for a Hals in 1907, unsuccessfully tried to buy it for $300,000. Thus, the 1926 purchase was a coup for Ringling and Böhler.

"The bigger the picture the smaller the price." [23]

Some misconceptions regarding Ringling's collecting style should be compared to auction house accounts of the day. The size, scale and theme of many works Ringling collected have at times led to the idea that by buying "big" he was buying what was cheapest and showiest. The sale of the large Rosa Bonheur canvas *Labourages Nivernais* is mentioned twice in Christie's 1929 season catalogue for the low price it fetched. This immense piece — it now occupies a whole wall in the Museum — had sold in 1884 for £410. Mitchell, the dealer from whom Ringling bought the piece, had paid a mere 46 guineas — roughly ten percent of the previous price. The auctioneers ascribed the dramatic drop in market value not only to changes in taste and fashion but to the fact that "few people have space for pictures of many square feet in dimension."[24]

The circumstances regarding Ringling's purchase, sometime between 1920 and 1931, of Jan Davidsz. de Heem's large *Still Life with Parrots* are still unknown (pl. 20). The masterwork has become a signature piece at the Ringling Museum, yet some considered de Heem unfashionable during Ringling's time. "Only very few people in this country want pictures of 'grub' hanging over their sideboards today," sniffed one British dealer.[25] The low prices paid for de Heem paintings during this period reflected their unpopularity. Most sold for under one hundred pounds. One large still life, similar in composition to the one in the Ringling collection, however, sold for £777 — nearly $4000 — in 1929.

The determination that works were "big" was relative. In a season catalogue from the times, Christie's claimed that a canvas of 5 1/2 by 4 1/2 feet was "far too much for the ordinary house and prohibitive to a flat."[26] Some of the criticism leveled against Ringling for his taste for big paintings, though, may have stemmed from confusion about his aims. Again, his plan to build a museum was generally eclipsed by his big-top reputation, and some evidently assumed his large paintings were for strictly private consumption. In fact, the immense scale of the pieces Ringling purchased could only

Figure 26. The second Holford Sale, at Christie's in London, May 15, 1928. John Ringling is identifiable to the right of auctioneer's podium. Julius Böhler may be to the left of podium.

have been accommodated in America by buildings especially constructed for them — buildings like the one John Phillips designed for the Ringling Museum. Ringling, in fact, did have one champion in the esteemed director of the Kaiser Friedrich Museum, Wilhelm von Bode. In a letter to Böhler in the Ringling Museum Archives, Bode expressed praise for Ringling who, "does not share a silly prejudice other Americans have...he does not object to large pictures."

The size versus quality issue was not raised at all when Ringling acquired the portrait of Philip IV by Don Diego de Silva y Velasquez (pl. 21). Ringling acquired this treasure at the second Holford sale in May of 1928. [27] A photograph of the sale in progress shows Ringling's usual inscrutable visage, unaware perhaps of the picture having been taken (fig. 26). Bidding was carried out by voice, a nod of the head or the blink of an eye. One can more easily imagine Ringling slightly inclining his head than bellowing a bid. For the showman's voice was in fact "low pitched, singularly soft, smooth as velvet" — hardly the bark of a ringmaster.[28] Böhler and Ringling attended this sale together, and the photograph shows a man who seems to be Böhler sitting opposite Ringling near the auctioneer's rostrum.

So positioned, the two men could communicate through eye contact or facial expression, yet would not have been too obviously recognized as a "team." In the second Holford sale, Ringling did personally bid on and buy pieces. Purchasing agents were utilized for eight of the 24 works Ringling marked for bidding. This small number may have made the elaborate strategy for concealing Ringling's identity deployed in the first Holford sale unnecessary.

Ringling personally bid on and purchased five paintings in the second Holford sale. Four of them sold for quite modest prices. The least expensive was an Andrea Schiavone for £31 10s, the most expensive, a Poussin for £157 10s. The prize piece for Ringling and for the Museum today was the Velasquez *Philip IV*. At this catalogue entry Ringling marked and circled a price of £3,300 and sales records reveal a purchase price of £3,456.

Ringling and Böhler stayed in London after the Holford sale and attended another at Sotheby's only a few days later. The next year's summer sales were the pinnacle of the post-war auction frenzy in the art world and the high point of John Ringling's personal collecting. The year also coincided with sea changes in Ringling's own personal and business life. Due first to business commitments and then to the general financial crisis, the funds available for Ringling's collecting activities rapidly dried up. He also remarried in 1930, and this second union seems to have had a destructive effect on his health, personal and financial circumstances. The number of artworks he is known to have purchased dropped by more than half from 1929 to 1930.   It fell to a mere handful in 1931.

> *I have never known a collector or a dealer who in his lifetime has given up*
> *voluntarily the pleasures of art-hunting.*[29]

Fewer Ringling auction catalogues exist from 1931 to 1936. Copies from 1935 and 1936 indicate, however, that Ringling continued to indulge his interest in art — virtually until the eve of his death. Repeated attacks of thrombosis in 1933 had partially paralyzed Ringling's right side, and despite a slow recovery, his mobility and even speech remained affected until his death. Estranged from most of his colleagues and business associates, he used his nephews John and Henry North as his business and personal aides. When the annotated catalogues reappear in 1936, they bear inscriptions similar to those of earlier years. A few contain what appear to be shorthand notations on the works, often followed by exclamation marks.

It is extremely doubtful that Ringling attended any auctions in 1935 or 1936. His personal appearance at the 1935 opening of the Circus in Madison Square Garden was staged by Ringling in order to prove that he was not incapacitated. His health and finances seemed to rally briefly in late

1935 and early 1936, perhaps tempting him with the hope of purchasing again. A 1935 headline from the front page of *Every Week in Sarasota County* asked: "Has John Ringling Regained Financial Power, Circus World?"[30]   The article claimed Ringling was "staging a financial and physical comeback."

Ringling had spent a great deal of energy in a relatively short span of time in order to build a major collection. Forced by events to give up "art-hunting," he could still read and mark his catalogues. Curiously, a work by Jean Jacques Henner that Ringling noted in a sale catalogue from March, 1936, is very similar to one of the first pieces bought by the Museum after Ringling's death. It seems fitting that just as Ringling himself purchased works he saw years earlier as a fledgling collector, the Museum he founded added to its store a piece quite like one he saw at the very end of his career as a connoisseur.

A Collection of Baroque Masterpieces

by Eric M. Zafran

Entering the first grand gallery of the John and Mable Ringling Museum of Art and coming into the presence of the enormous Rubens tapestry cartoons is an experience unparalleled in American museums. Further on, in the large gallery of Italian Baroque paintings, the visitor can not help but be struck by the size, the radiant colors and the vivid images of the portraits and religious scenes. Their grandiosity and immediacy are the essence of Baroque art, as John Ringling understood well. The German dealer Julius Böhler, Ringling's chief advisor and agent during the acquisition of the Museum collection, recalled that he and Ringling initially

> bought whatever pictures we thought were good and right in price. . . . and in time
> we conceived the idea of concentrating our energies on buying Baroque pictures. . . .
> We bought a great number of these with the result that today already the Sarasota
> museum is the richest in Baroque paintings in the states.[1]

Since Böhler wrote these words in the late 1940s, other notable collections of Italian Baroque art have been formed in America.[2] Some can perhaps boast greater individual masterpieces, but none can rival the Ringling's comprehensive holdings in seventeenth century Italian paintings.

For a collector intent on quickly creating a major museum, the combination mentioned by Böhler was a winning one. Those of Ringling's contemporaries who collected Italian art pursued chaste early gold ground panels, works by Renaissance masters like Raphael and Titian or the later decorative canvases of the Venetian school. With characteristic boldness, Ringling went his own way and had his greatest success with art of the seventeenth century. The artists whose works he rapidly acquired between 1924 and 1931 had for the most part fallen from favor. They often came from noble English collections. He began with purchases from the 1924 sale of the Duke of Westminster collection in London. These were a Sassoferrato *Madonna and Child* and a *Three Marys at the Sepulchre* attributed to Salvator Rosa, which turned out to be a copy. An authentic and very important Rosa from the Westminster collection — then believed to be a self portrait, but now titled an *Allegory of Study* — was acquired for Ringling in 1925.

The next major Italian Baroque acquisition came in 1926, with the purchase of a great portrait then attributed to Maratta but later assigned to Sassoferrato. The disposal by Christie's of the renowned Holford collection in two installments — in 1927 and 1928 — was a bonanza for Ringling. There, he acquired the core of his Italian Baroque collection — and also some problematic works. In the masterwork category were a Rosa landscape, two Carlo Dolcis and several by Annibale Carracci. Two of these works are now known to be by Domenico Fiasella, the *St. John in the Wilderness* is now ascribed to Francesco Albani, the *Susanna and the Elders* to Sisto Badalocchio, and a Guercino is now assigned to Benedetto Gennari.

In early 1929, Ringling bought a Cavaliere d'Arpino at the Metropolitan Museum of Art sale. Later that year he returned to London for the Earl of Yarborough sale. There, Ringling bought his one authentic Guercino, the large *Annunciation*, as well as two Francesco Molas, a Luca Giordano, a school of Pietro da Cortona and another Rosa landscape. Two supposed Guido Renis were later found to be copies by other artists including Sirani. This is also the case with two Caravaggios purchased by Ringling.

These last were among works Ringling purchased individually from a variety of sources, many still unidentified. In this category are such Italian Baroque paintings as the Artemesia Gentileschi *St. Cecilia*, Onorio Marinari's *Martyr Saint*, a pair of Marco Ricci landscapes with religious scenes, the Luca Giordano *Adoration*, Pietro Novelli's *St. John on Patmos*, a Francesco Solimena, Massimo Stanzione's *Rest on the Flight* and the Andrea Vaccaro *St. John the Baptist*. Other works of distinction bought individually include the Pietro da Cortona *Hagar and the Angel* (pl. 22), acquired from the dealer-scholar Vitale Bloch in 1931, and the Luca Giordano *Flight into Egypt*.

During the time Ringling was active, there was little first rate Italian Baroque art to be seen in America. French writer René Brimo, in his thorough 1938 overview of American taste in collecting, points out that this may have been due to a strain of artistic Puritanism in this country that looked askance at the nudity so often found in religious and mythological subjects of the Italian Baroque. As collections willing to resist this prejudice, Brimo cites Ringling's and that of the

University of Notre Dame.[3] The latter did have a modest number of Italian Baroque works from the Braschi Collection in Rome,[4] but does not compare to Ringling's survey of the major Italian schools of the seventeenth century.

There had in fact been some small pockets of Italian Baroque art in various collections around America formed in the late nineteenth century, such as those at Georgetown University, the Bryan Collection given to the New York Historical Society, the Isaac Lea collection in Philadelphia, Thomas Walker in Minneapolis, and E.B. Crocker in Sacramento.[5] The major museums of New York, Boston, Cleveland, Chicago, and St. Louis had only limited representation of Italian Baroque before the 1920s. The Detroit Institute of Arts, through a gift from the Scripps family, appears to have had the greatest number, but many of its holdings were not authentic.[6] A major change in taste among knowledgeable museum professionals occurred, however, after the first great exhibition of Italian Baroque painting was held in Florence in 1922. This show demonstrated the quality and power of these long-neglected masters, and during the remainder of the decade the Metropolitan Museum of Art and the Cleveland Museum both acquired works by Bernardo Strozzi, the museum in Minneapolis gained notable pictures by Guido Reni and Guercino and Rochester's museum picked up a Fetti. The Fogg Art Museum at Harvard, where Arthur McComb in the Fine Arts department promoted the Baroque period and organized the first American exhibition of Italian Baroque art in early 1929, received one supposed Caravaggio as a gift in 1922 and purchased another in 1929.[7]

Still, there were few private collectors in the first decades of the twentieth century for Italian Baroque art. The most aggressive acquisitor of the era was William Randolph Hearst, who in the course of decorating his various palatial residences did obtain several Italian Baroque works. Some of these are still on view at his California estate at San Simeon, and others were later given to the Los Angeles County Museum of Art.[8] There was only one other collector in America who understood the Italian Baroque and to whom Ringling might have looked for inspiration. This was Henry Walters of Baltimore. Walters, who had inherited the basis of a great collection from his father, sought to expand his holdings of European paintings and in 1902 purchased an enormously varied Roman collection of Italian paintings that was especially rich in the great names of the Baroque.[9] He, too, was creating an essentially encyclopedic — if idiosyncratic — collection, to be housed as a public resource in an Italian-style palazzo. It is unknown whether Ringling ever visited Walters, but in one of the very few articles published on his museum before it opened, Ringling named the Baltimore collector as one of the distinguished connoisseurs and scholars on his board of directors.[10] This group does not seem to have ever been assembled.

Ringling, as Böhler attested, had become extremely knowledgeable. It is difficult to think of another American collector in the 1920s who could identify, let alone research, a putative Ludovico Carracci. But this is precisely what Ringling did in a 1929 letter to Böhler. With regard to the large painting which he had acquired as an Annibale Carracci at the Holford sale, he wrote:

> *I think I found out why they attribute the Caracci [sic], "Christ healing the blind" to*
> *Ludovico. I presume you have* Storia Della Pittura Italian, *Second Edition,*
> *Volume Six. On page seven, you will find "Christ healing the blind" illustrated,*
> *attributed to Ludovico.[11]*

That the painting (pl. 24) was later more correctly attributed to the Genoese born painter Fiasella is less important than the collector's obvious commitment to the detective work involved in connoisseurship.

While the name Carracci interested few collectors in this period, the greats of Northern Baroque painting - Rubens, Rembrandt, Hals, Van Dyck and a handful of others — continued to function as status symbols. This trend is confirmed by the briefest look at the collections formed by Gardner in Boston; by Frick, Morgan, Altman and Bache in New York; by Taft in Cincinnatti; Epstein in Chicago; Johnson in Philadelphia; or by Widener whose holdings went to the National Gallery of Art in Washington, D.C.. Thus when Ringling pursued such popular works, he often had to pay high prices. This was the case, for example, with his Frans Hals portrait. And when he attempted to seek bargains or indulged in "a little sport,"[12] he was not always successful. This was notably true of the various Rembrandts he purchased — all of which did not in the end prove to be by the master. But Ringling certainly succeeded with the huge examples of Rubens and Snyders, for few other collectors could even consider works so large. The great German museum director Wilhelm von Bode justifiably praised Ringling's independence in going against the taste of the day to buy these outsized and sexy works.[13]

Nor should it be overlooked that in the course of his short collecting career, Ringling actually amassed a very fine representative group of seventeenth century Northern Baroque paintings. His collection — which covers all the standard categories of history subjects, portraiture, genre, still life, landscape, and interiors — includes examples by David Teniers, Jacob Ruysdael, Jan Steen, Paulus Potter, Juriaen van Streeck and Nicolas Maes, as well as a superb Jan Davidsz. de Heem. In addition, Ringling showed a willingness to acquire offbeat Northern Baroque works, including an *Allegorical Portrait* by Gerbrand van der Eeckhout, a Brazilian landscape by Frans Post, Arnold Houbraken's *Dido and Aeneas*, an allegory by Jacob de Wit and, most especially, the Italianate *Hagar and Ishmael* by the Dutch artist Karel Dujardin (pl. 25).

As for the other schools of Baroque painting, Ringling could be equally adventurous. Several collectors, most notably Archer Huntington — who founded the Hispanic Society in New York[14] — competed for Spanish masterpieces, and Ringling joined them in pursuing works attributed to such well known artists as Bartolomé Esteban Murillo, Jusepe de Ribera (pl. 26) and Francisco Zurburan. Yet he also found room for the more unusual artists Alonso Cano, Juan de Valdes Leal and Juan de Pareja. In French art, Ringling purchased standard classics — a large Poussin, two Gaspar Dughets and a supposed Claude Lorrain. But he also bought a fine Simon Vouet (pl. 27) and, even more remarkably, the set of the *Seven Acts of Mercy* by Sebastian Bourdon. There were also a rare work by Jacques Stella purchased as a Le Sueur and a *St. Bruno* supposed to be a Hyacinthe Rigaud but now identified as a copy by Claude Mellan.

Recognition of Ringling's achievement was sporadic and slow in coming. This was ostensibly due to Sarasota's isolated location and later to the ten year closing of the museum after Ringling's death. Nevertheless, there were short notes on acquisitions, which appeared in various scholarly periodicals. These articles, perhaps encouraged by Böhler's connections to German specialists, included a 1928 notice and illustration in *Pantheon* treating the supposed Rembrandt *Evangelist*.[15] In the following year the Spanish expert August L. Mayer wrote about Ringling's Ribera in *International Studio*.[16] In 1930, *The Art Digest* announced "Ringling Buys a Rubens" and put the large *Pausias and Glycera* on its front cover,[17] and Wilhem Valentiner published the Frans Hals portrait in 1935.[18] Mentions of the collection in scholarly publications continued through the 1930s.

One of the clearest indications of the repute attained by Ringling's Baroque collection within the art profession was a letter of inquiry which the young art historian and museum director A. Everett Austin sent to Ringling in New York in November of 1929. As director of the Wadsworth Atheneum from 1927 to 1945, Austin made that institution into the leading American museum for the acquisition and exhibition of Baroque art. He became the director of the John and Mable Ringling Museum in 1946. "My dear Mr. Ringling," he wrote in 1929:

> *Mr. Forbes, of the Fogg Art Museum, whose assistant I was at Harvard for some*
> *years, has told me that you have many very fine paintings of the Baroque period,*
> *and I am wondering if you would possibly be willing to lend me some of these for*
> *our exhibition.[19]*

Edward Forbes had visited the Ringling Museum earlier that year and must have reported its contents to Austin.[20] Unfortunately there is no known response from Ringling or Böhler, and as it turned out no works were lent,[21] perhaps due to the necessity of having all of them on hand for what Ringling hoped was to be the imminent public opening of the museum. Nevertheless, the Wadsworth Atheneum followed Ringling in creating a significant holding of Baroque paintings by many of the same artists.

The other American collection which was ultimately to become significant in its Baroque holdings was that of Samuel H. Kress. Here, too, there is a personnel link to the Ringling Museum, for Kress's chief advisor from 1941 was Dr. William Suida, who in 1949 prepared the first published catalogue of the Ringling collection. In his catalogue introduction, Suida noted the specific strength of Ringling's Italian Baroque works:

> *The seventeenth century collection which contains numerous examples by the leading*
> *artists of the Bolognese, Roman and Neapolitan Schools (not forgetting the fine*
> *Venetian and Lombard pictures) has no equal in this hemisphere. Where else indeed*
> *may one find such superb pictures by the Carracci, Guido Reni, Mola, Guercino,*
> *Dolci, Furini, Sassoferrato, Massimo Stanzioni, Salvator Rosa, Cavallino and Luca*
> *Giordano, and in such abundance?[22]*

The sentiment was seconded by several other writers in the late 1940s and early 1950s. The print connoisseur A. Hyatt Mayor wrote in 1948:
"Probably no collection outside Europe gives so rich an idea of taste from 1600 to 1800 ".[23]

The 1950 *Art News Annual* was devoted to "The Baroque and the Circus." It featured a general article on "The Baroque" by Austin that included the first color reproductions of Regnieri's *St. Matthew Writing the Gospel* and Dolci's *Blue Madonna*. In the other major article, "John Ringling's Greatest Show," the magazine's editor, Alfred Frankfurter, described Ringling's achievement as "the leading American collection of Baroque and Rococo paintings."[24]

The English connoisseur Osbert Sitwell also visited Sarasota in the early 1950s and in a very admiring essay noted that the museum differed from "most public collections which lack personality." He went on to write that the explanation for the Ringling Museum's

> *liveliness and character which separates it so vividly from the ordinary run of musty,*
> *echoing buildings dedicated to the instruction of the public is that the collection and*
> *the edifice which enshrine it were for long the aim and finally the creation of one*
> *man... who was plainly a man of immense individuality with his own ideas on*

many subjects. In addition the Gallery is lucky enough to have ensconced in this last
pocket of the Baroque and Rococo one of the most original minded and imaginative
of all museum directors Mr. A. Everett Austin, Jr.[25]

A decade later another Englishman, W.G. Constable, gave his observation of the Ringling Museum in his classic study of American collecting:

...with the seventeenth and eighteenth century Italian masters, the group of
Bolognese, Neopolitan, Roman, and Venetian painters of that period is perhaps the
most important in the United States.[26]

That importance was acknowledged the following year in the most significant American exhibition of Italian Baroque art to date, held at the Detroit Institute of Art. There, the leading scholar of the subject, Rudolf Wittkower, acknowledged the John and Mable Ringling Museum, along with the Wadsworth Atheneum, as the most important public sources of such works.[27]

This judgment received further international confirmation in a 1966 article by the Louvre's knowledgeable curator Pierre Rosenberg, who further described the Ringling Museum as one of "ces anomalies baroque dont l'Amerique a le secret." He also ventured that Ringling bought his unfashionable Baroque canvases out of a "sincere love of the period which corresponded perfectly to his temperament as a man of the theater."[28]

Paintings from the Ringling's collection continued to have a role in loan exhibitions around the world, and in 1986 the exhibition entitled *Baroque Paintings from the John and Mable Ringling Museum of Art* toured America. It was welcomed at the National Gallery of Art in Washington, D.C., where Chief Curator and noted authority on Italian painting Sydney J. Freedberg described it as "a standard we should like to meet here."[29]

Plate 1.
J.H. Phillips
*Detail of watercolor/drawing
of Museum east entrance facade*
1928
22 x 16 1/2 inches

Plate 2.

J.H. Phillips, earliest existing blueprint for Museum, dated September, 1926,
58 x 39 1/2 inches. Note Museum is referred to as "the John Ringling
Museum of Art." In this month, Cà d'Zan Architect Dwight James Baum
was nearing completion of his design of "Residence for Mrs. John Ringling."

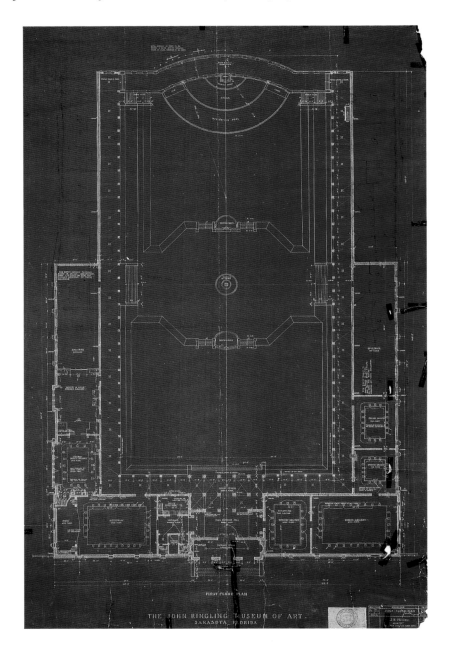

Plate 3.
J.H. Phillips, early blueprint for "the John Ringling Museum of Art," showing
front elevation and through-court cross section looking east toward entrance,
September, 1926, 40 x 19 1/2 inches. Note front facade is pierced by eight
windows, never executed. Statuary drawn in niches were never installed, and
central entrance arch is drawn slightly higher than two flanking arches.

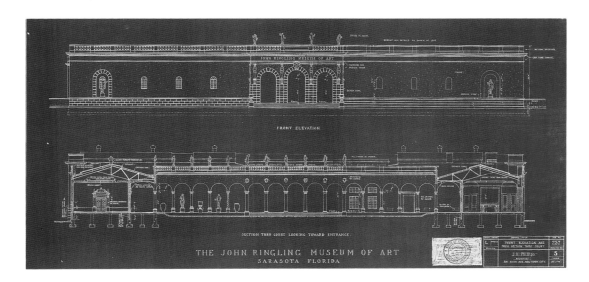

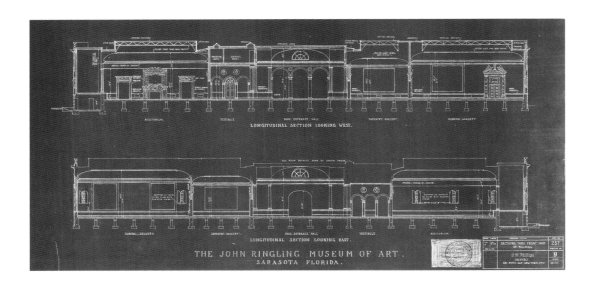

Plate 4.
J.H. Phillips, blueprint of Museum showing longitudinal section looking west
and east, September, 1926, 40 x 19 1/2 inches. Note interior shutters for
windows never executed on east facade.

Plate 5.
Bernardino Luini
**The Madonna Enthroned
with the Child
between St. Sebastian
and St. Roch**
Oil on panel
circa 1507-32
69 x 61 1/2 inches

Plate 6.
Peter Paul Rubens and Studio (figures)
and Osias Beert the Elder (flowers)
**Pausias and Glycera
(A Scholar Inspired by Nature)**
Oil on canvas
circa 1612-15
80 x 76 1/2 inches

Plate 7.
Giovanni Antonio Fasolo
Portrait of a Family Group
Oil on canvas
circa 1561-65
86 x 71 inches

Plate 8.
Alvaro di Piero
The Angel of the Annunciation
Tempera, gold ground on panel
after 1428
50 1/4 x 18 3/8 inches

Plate 9.
Alvaro di Piero
The Virgin of the Annunciation
Tempera, gold ground on panel
after 1428
50 x 18 5/8 inches

Plate 16.
Paolo Veronese
The Rest on the Flight into Egypt
Oil on canvas
circa 1566-68
92 1/4 x 63 1/4 inches

Plate 17.
Studio of Rembrandt van Rijn
Lamentation
Oil on canvas
late 1640s
71 x 78 1/4 inches

Plate 18.
Joshua Reynolds
Portrait of the Marquis of Granby
Oil on canvas
1766
96 5/8 x 82 inches

Plate 19.
Frans Hals
Pieter Jacobsz. Olycan
Oil on canvas
circa 1639
43 1/4 x 34 inches

Plate 20.
Jan Davidsz. de Heem
Still Life with Parrots
Oil on canvas
late 1640s
59 1/4 x 45 1/2 inches

Plate 21.
Don Diego de Silva y Velasquez
Philip IV
Oil on canvas
circa 1625-35
82 3/8 x 47 5/8 inches

Plate 22.
Pietro da Cortona
Hagar and the Angel
Oil on canvas
circa 1637
45 x 58 3/4 inches

Plate 23.
Gaudenzio Ferrari
The Holy Family with a Donor
Oil on panel
late 1520s
60 1/2 x 45 1/2 inches
John Ringling aquired this work at the
first Holford sale, in 1927.

Plate 24.
Domenico Fiasella, ***Christ Healing the Blind***
Oil on canvas, circa 1615-16, 109 5/8 x 71 7/8 inches
This painting was offered at the 1928 Holford sale as an Annibale Carracci. Ringling,
however, based on his research in Giovanni Rosini's art historical text *Storia della pittura
italiani eposta coi monumenti*, believed it was the work of Ludovico Carracci.

Plate 25.
Karel Dujardin
Hagar and Ishmael
Oil on canvas
circa 1662
73 3/4 x 55 inches

Plate 26.
Jusepe de Ribera
Madonna and Child
Oil on canvas
1643
43 3/4 x 39 1/2 inches

Plate 27.
Simon Vouet
Mars and Venus
Oil on canvas
circa 1640
57 1/2 x 42 1/2 inches

Plate 28.
Page from the 1913 facsimile of the Gutenberg Bible published by Insel-Verlag in Leipzig, one of a limited edition of 300 copies. Ringling's copy was given to him and inscribed by Otto H.F. Vollbehr, a noted collector of incunabula.

Plate 29.
Color lithograph from Ringling's copy of *Le Costume historique*, published in Paris in 1876, depicting sixteenth century European costumed figures and with captions in three languages. The women represented include Catherine de'Medici and other historical figures.

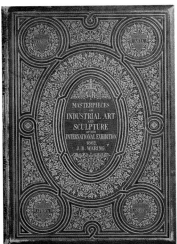

Plate 30.
Color lithograph from Ringling's copy of William Beebe's rare *The Monograph of the Pheasants.*

Plate 31.
One of the numerous hand tooled and gold embossed leather bound volumes in Ringling's library.

Plate 32.
Jean-Baptiste-Edouard Detaille, **The Retreat**
Oil on canvas, 1873, 49 x 63 inches

Plate 33.
Ferdinand Roybet, **The Connoisseurs**
Oil on canvas, 1876, 48 x 59 inches

Plate 41.
After Guido Reni
David with the Head of Goliath
Oil on canvas
after 1605
90 1/4 x 68 inches

Plate 42.
Peter Paul Rubens
Achilles Dipped into the River Styx
Oil on panel
after 1630
43 1/16 x 35 5/16 inches

Plate 43.
Jan Fyt
Atalanta and Meleager
Hunt the Calydonian Boar
Oil on canvas
1648
96 x 162 inches

Plate 44.
Nöel-Nicolas Coypel
Madame de Bourbon-Conti
Oil on canvas
1731
54 1/8 x 41 7/8 inches

Plate 45.
Antoine Pesne
Portrait of Philippine Charlotte,
Princess of Prussia
Oil on canvas
after 1736
57 1/2 x 44 inches

Plate 40.
Isaak Luttichuys
Portrait of a Man with a Spear
Oil on canvas
circa 1660
37 1/4 x 31 inches
In 1981 , the Ringling Museum added
the pendant to this portrait to its collection.

Plate 47.
Alfred Stevens
Young Lady in a White Dress
Oil on panel
1879
21 1/2 x 17 3/4 inches
This was the only painting that hung in
Mable Ringling's bedroom, in the Cà d'Zan.

Plate 48.
Savely Sorine
Portrait of Mable Ringling
Watercolor on paper
1927
36 1/2 x 29 1/2 inches

Plate 49.
Savely Sorine
Portrait of John Ringling
Watercolor on paper
1927
61 1/2 x 44 1/2 inches

The Library

The Education of a Connoisseur

by Linda R. McKee

The library of The John and Mable Ringling Museum of Art is an enduring testament to John Ringling's passion for collecting. His love for Italian and Northern Baroque art as well as the decorative arts is reflected not only in his art collection and the magnificent Italian villa-like museum designed to house it, but also in the books he acquired in his lifetime. Much about Ringling as a collector can be learned from his original library. Indeed, his book collection can be seen as a complement to his art museum and as a tool in realizing his dream of building one. Comparison with highly respected bibliographies reveals that Ringling had assembled a remarkably comprehensive library in a discipline that was then very much in its infancy.

In his Last Will and Testament, John Ringling bequeathed to the State of Florida his art museum and residence, including the "library of art books" contained in them.[1] After his death in 1936, Ringling's personal library of nearly 1,500 books was found distributed among the bedroom, office, and living room of Cà d' Zan, his residence on Sarasota Bay; an office in the Museum; and a fireproof storeroom on the estate grounds. These titles were included in the 1937 estate inventory appraised after his death under the supervision of Jonce McGurk (with the assistance of book appraiser Albert Langer) and listed in the bequest to the State of Florida. About 28 pages of this inventory — within the section labeled "Furniture in John Ringling Home" — contain the titles and volumes of books found in Ringling's Cà d'Zan office, on shelves in Ringling's office closet, in a bookcase in an anteroom to the office, and in the downstairs living room. Other pages list "Books in Library Store House (Garage)" and books found in the Museum office. The whereabouts or fate of many of the books listed on the store house inventory pages is not known. Hundreds of titles in literature and history are simply gone. Significantly, however, more than 500 titles from John Ringling's art book collection do survive.

Ten years later in 1946, upon the settlement of the Ringling estate and transfer of the Museum and Cà d'Zan and its collections to the State of Florida, this collection of art books, as well as a few remaining titles of literature and miscellaneous subjects, was officially accessioned into what would eventually become the Art Museum library. Maud L. Dean, the Museum's first librarian from 1946 to 1953, began the library's first accession book. Each volume in the new library was assigned an accession number, a system still carried on today for every book added to the library. This early accession book survives today and aids library staff in taking the inventory of what has come to be known as the original John Ringling Library. At the time, the librarian also made ink notations on the title page of each volume and listed its assigned value, the year (1946 or 1947), and the accession number. Another bibliography of the "John Ringling Library" by a later librarian has been preserved and is also used in taking the inventory of the collection. The McGurk inventory, these two lists, and the original typed cards from the library's card catalogue have been used in the present account. Originally, the books were catalogued in a seldom used classification system modeled after the celebrated Frick Art Reference Library in New York. Since the early 1980s, many volumes in the library, including most of the original John Ringling library, have been recatalogued according to the standard Library of Congress classification system and entered electronically into the OCLC database. The contents of the OCLC database (and thus the holdings of the Ringling library) are available to libraries and scholars internationally. An on-line computerized card catalogue provides present day library users in the Art Museum with the contents of the library at the touch of a few keystrokes. Ringling could not envision that his small private treasury of books, now numbering over 50,000 items, would develop into one of the most important art history collections in the state of Florida, encompassing books, periodicals, videotapes, CD-ROMs of some of the world's greatest art collections, on-line databases and Internet access.

It is not clear if John Ringling ever intended to build a library in the Art Museum. The Cà d'Zan had no formal library, though there were glass-encased book shelves in Ringling's bedroom and office. Perhaps he had such a vision in mind when, in 1926, he purchased several interiors from the Astor residence in New York — including its fine oak-paneled library, later installed as Gallery 20 in the Art Museum. After the state assumed ownership of Ringling's collections, this gallery was temporarily turned into a library to house his books. A recently found typed manuscript written by Frances Cheney Hoersting, the Museum librarian from 1959 to 1964 and secretary to the Museum board, describes the library in this early location:

Mable Ringling intended this oak room to be a sort of reception room, adjacent to

the Auditorium. . . . Mr. Ringling's collection of about 500 books on art found their

way here, and it is now used as the Library. As such, it is the largest art research

library in the South. There are now some 5000 volumes and bound periodicals

dealing with all phases of art and art history, with particular emphasis on the

period which appealed to Mr. Ringling so much — the Baroque. Some of the books

are extremely rare and date back to the early days of printing. The collection is open

to the public for research, but no books may leave the premises.[2]

The growing library would remain in this location for twenty years. Upon completion of the addition of the west galleries in 1966, it was moved to the third floor of this new wing, where it remains. Helen Strader, Museum librarian from 1964-65 recalls retrieving uncatalogued books (possibly more of Ringling's collection), with Craig Rubadoux, then on the Museum staff, from a storage area above Gallery 20 and accessioning them into the collection.[3]

Ringling did intend that a library be included in an art school planned as an extension of the north gallery wing. This library was to be distinct from his personal collection. The "Bulletin of the School of Fine and Applied Art of the John and Mable Ringling Art Museum," issued in 1931 in conjunction with Southern College, lauds the planned school's library as a large collection of reference books, text books and fiction "catalogued in accordance with the most improved methods, and a trained librarian is in charge. The collection includes specially selected books on art."[4] As the school never opened as planned on the Museum grounds, neither the source nor the present location of the books (if they were in fact collected) is known.

Ringling apparently did have a "library" in one of his New York residences, but little record of its contents exists. Taylor Gordon, Ringling's manservant, mentions it in his 1929 memoir, *Born to Be*: "I went down to the Fifth Avenue apartment, and he had me come in the library."[5] In the same memoir, however, Gordon declares that, "It is surprising how much [John Ringling] knows about the world, yet seldom you catch him reading any books."[6] And after Ringling's death, a list of contents of his Park Avenue residence did include some books. A 1940 document lists, under the heading "Received from Armstrong Transfer the following items, being miscellaneous items withheld from auction of John Ringling's possessions from New York Warehouses," 14 volumes of books and "several photos and art catalogues."[7] Some of these same titles do appear on the McGurk inventory.

In any case, John Ringling's taste in books was not guided by the goals and interests of the wealthy and prolific art and book collectors of the time— John Pierpont Morgan, John Jacob Astor, Harry Elkins Widener, Henry E. Huntington, or Robert Hoe III, the latter one of our country's greatest book collectors. The tales of the madness and desire of the great book collectors in the beginning of this century are no less harrowing than those of the great art collectors. Ringling, however, did not purchase his books to showcase them — he bought them *to learn*. He relied on his art books and journals for an astoundingly quick self-education on the artists and schools of art which most interested him, in order to become an informed art collector.

Documentation concerning the amassment of Ringling's art collection and its provenance continues to grow, but much less is known about how, where and from whom Ringling acquired his personal art library. It is known that he purchased some of his volumes from auctions of private libraries at the Anderson Galleries on Park Avenue in New York and at Christie, Manson & Woods in London. These included the 1927 sale of the library of Dr. John E. Stillwell and the 1928 sale of the Mrs. Eugenie K. Cunningham library — both in New York.[8] Other of Ringling's books can be traced back to a 1927 London sale of the Carpenter Garnier collection.[9] The catalogues of these sales, as well as many of the original auction house catalogues Ringling used in the acquisition of his art collection, were originally housed in the Museum library but were transferred, between 1991 and 1993, to the newly established Archives of The John and Mable Ringling Museum of Art.

Almost no primary documentation exists relating to the purchase or acquisition of Ringling's books. A few exceptions have recently been discovered. Two letters from 1929 were recently acquired by the Archives. One is from a book dealer, Hans Goltz of Munich, who writes to Ringling's art dealer, Julius Böhler, in Lucerne, asking for settlement of Ringling's two-year-old outstanding bill of 969.35 marks. A list of the ten titles and book sets in question is attached. The second letter, from

Goltz to Böhler and dated just two days later, thanks Böhler for settling the account. The books are still in the library today. A receipt for customs requirements made out to Böhler by London bookseller James Bain was found in Ringling's copy of a rare 1775 book, James Adair's, *The history of the American Indians: particularly those nations adjoining to the Mississippi East and West Florida...containing an account of their origin, language, manners..*, providing further evidence that Böhler purchased not only art for Ringling but books as well.

Aside from these exceptions, the books themselves yield few clues about their former owners. Only a very small number are inscribed as gifts to Ringling. And with the exception of some of his art journals — such as *The Magazine of Art*, *The Burlington Magazine*, and *Connoisseur* — there are almost no pencil or pen markings in Ringling's hand in any of them. The limited notations that do exist are in most cases markings made by succeeding librarians during cataloguing efforts.

With regard to the quality of Ringling's library, one need only turn to professionally accepted and standard bibliographies of art history compiled during the twentieth century. Foremost among these is E. Louise Lucas' 1952 *The Harvard List of Books on Art* — an attempt, according to its author, "to select a few thousand titles basic to the study of art history."[10] Also respected are Mary W. Chamberlain's 1959 *Guide to Art Reference Books*; Lucas' 1968 *Art Books: A Basic Bibliography on the Fine Arts*; Etta Arntzen & Robert Rainwater's 1980 Guide to the Literature of Art History; and one of the most recent lists, Wolfgang Freitag's 1985 *Art Books: A Basic Bibliography of Monographs on Artists*.

Freitag asserts that the core of every art book collection is the artist monograph. Ringling's library does not contradict this opinion. Monographs on over forty-five individual artists — including Botticelli, Bellini, Raphael, Andrea del Sarto, Giorgione, Rembrandt, Rubens, Van Dyck, Poussin, Tiepolo, Veronese, Dürer, Altdorfer and Tintoretto — were found in his office. Many of these are listed by Freitag as still-important works. Books found on English artists include studies of Turner, Ward, Romney, Gainsborough, Constable, Burne-Jones and Raeburn. Inside a bookcase in Ringling's bedroom were titles on Cellini, Correggio, Pintoricchio, Piero della Francesca, Signorelli, Francia, Mantegna and Rubens. Interestingly, Ambroise Vollard's classic work on Paul Cézanne was among those found in the private sleeping chamber. Julius Meier-Gräfe's Degas study was found in the office closet, as was his biography of Van Gogh.

There can be no doubt that Italian painting was dear to John Ringling's heart. He owned many still-classic surveys of Italian art, and several volumes of one — Raimond van Marle's, *The Development of the Italian Schools of Painting*, published in The Hague from 1923 to 1938 — were found in his bedroom. The remaining van Marle volumes were found in a closet off his office that also contained other seminal studies of Italian art. Fourteen volumes of Adolfo Venturi's *Storia dell'arte italiana* were found in the museum office. Both Chamberlain and Arntzen cite Venturi's monumental work — which treats painting, sculpture and architecture from the early Christian period to the sixteenth century — as one of the most important studies of Italian painting, if not, indeed, "the definitive history of Italian art."[11] Ringling also owned J.A. Crowe's and G.B. Cavcaselle's early standard survey of Central Italian painting, *A History of Painting in Italy: Umbria, Florence and Siena from the Second to the Sixteenth Century* (1903-1914), and *A History of Painting in North Italy: Venice, Padua, Vicenza* (1912).

It is also not surprising that Ringling was well acquainted with the writings of one of his contemporaries, Bernard Berenson, a leading authority then and still today on Italian schools of art. Included in his library were Berenson's *Neapolitan Painting of the Seicento*; *The Venetian Painters of the Renaissance*; *North Italian Painters of the Renaissance*; *The Central Italian Painters of the Renaissance*; *Venetian Painting in America*; and *The Study and Criticism of Italian Art*. All were found in a bookcase in Ringling's office closet.

Ringling also owned and apparently consulted Giovanni Rosini's *Storia della Pittura Italiana Esposta coi Monumenti* (*History of Painting in Italy Illustrated by its Monuments*, published in Pisa from 1848 to 1852). This book was cited by Ringling in a letter to Böhler concerning the attribution of a painting. (See Eric Zafran's essay on A Collection of Baroque Masterpieces in this volume.)

Italian art surveys were by no means Ringling's only interest. He also owned important titles in Northern European painting. These included Max J. Friedländer's *Die Altniederländische Malerei*, an important work on early Dutch painting that even the great art historian Erwin Panofsky praised as "one of the few uncontested masterpieces produced by our discipline."[12] Ringling also owned a volume published in honor of Friedländer, a Festschrift entitled, Zum 60. *Geburtstag Max J. Friedländer (For Max J. Friedländer's Sixtieth Birthday)*. Friedländer was one of seven men Ringling originally named to be director of his newly established art museum. August L. Mayer was another. Mayer authored three books in Ringling's library: *Mittelalterliche Plastik in Italien (Medieval Sculpture in Italy,1923)*, *Francisco de Goya (1929)* and *Dominico Theotocopuli El Greco (1926)*. Among the El Greco works reproduced in the latter volume is *Christ on the Cross*; John Ringling purchased the painting for his Museum just two years after the book's publication.

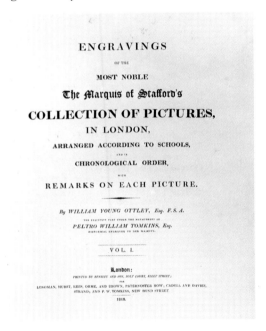

Figure 27. Title page of Ringling's 1818 volume of engravings of the Marquis of Stafford's collection of pictures, one of many art books he acquired in order to study the contents of the great English collections.

Other art surveys included in his collection were Sir William Stirling-Maxwell's limited edition of the *Annals of the Artists of Spain* (40 out of 650 copies), John Smith's 1829-1842 *A Catalogue raisonné of the works of the most eminent Dutch, Flemish and French painters*, an important early work that Arntzen identifies as the basis for Hofstede de Groot's monumental catalogue published in the following century.[13] Georg Gottfried Dehio's *Geschichte der deutschen Kunst* — the "standard German history of German art covering from the beginning through the nineteenth and twentieth centuries" according to Chamberlain[14] — is also in Ringling's collection. Dehio's volumes were among those listed in Goltz's 1929 itemized bill to Böhler. So, too, were the Festschrift to Max Friedländer and the multi-volume *Propyläen-Kunstegeschichte*, a history of art series heralded and unsurpassed in its time, the strength of which for us today lies in its "lavish illustrations-some in color-which form a unique body of visual material."[15]

The Ringling book collection also contained other classic art history texts still consulted and cited today by art historians and scholars. These include Giorgio Vasari's *Lives of the Most Eminent*

Figure 28. After Andrea del Sarto, *The Madonna Della Scala*, sixteenth century. Oil on panel, 72 x 52 inches. This painting was one of many acquired by Ringling at the 1927 sale of works from the Duke of Holford collection by Christie's in London.

Painters, Sculptors and Architects in a limited edition published in London for the Medici Society from 1912 to 1915, and a 1881 edition of Johann Winckelmann's *History of Ancient Art*.

A large part of the library consisted of art collection catalogues. Some document sales actually attended by Böhler, Ringling or Joseph Duveen. Numerous hand-notated auction catalogues from Anderson Galleries in New York have been transferred to the museum archives, but many substantial and handsome limited edition catalogues remain in the Ringling Museum library today. They include *The Wallace collection (paintings) at Hertford House*; *The Adolph Lewisohn collection of modern French paintings and sculptures*; Robert Benson's *Catalogue of Italian pictures at 16 South Street, Park Lane, London and Buchhurst in Sussex*; *A catalogue of some of the paintings of the British School in the collection of Henry Edwards Huntington at San Marino, California*; *Collection Spiridon de Rome: Catalogue des Tableaux des Ecoles Italiennes des XIVe et XVe Siècles*; *Collections Marczell von Nemes: Catalogue des Tableaux*; and Evelyn and Arthur Wellesley Wellington's *A Descriptive and Historical Catalogue of the Collection of Pictures and Sculpture at Apsley House*.

The three volumes of *The Holford Collection, Dorchester House*, published in 1924 and 1927, are exceptional not only for their craftsmanship but also for their importance to the history of the Ringling art collection. The Holford sales were "examples of a phenomenon peculiar to the present era — the extinction of great private collections of works of art."[16] Ringling's copy of the 1924 volume, was from a limited edition of 300. The 1927 volumes were printed in a limited run of 400 and are signed by their editor, Robert Benson. Ringling purchases from the 1927 and 1928 Holford sales include Diego Velasquez's portrait of Philip IV (pl. 21); Andrea del Sarto's *Vision of St. Matthew* (fig.28), now attributed to "after del Sarto" and renamed *The Madonna della Scala*; Gaudenzio Ferrari's *The Holy Family With Donor*(pl. 23); Sisto Baldalocchio's *Susannah and the Elders*; *The Blue Madonna* (after Carlo Dolci); *A Sultana of Venice* (now attributed to "after Titian" and entitled *La Sultana Rossa*); Edward Burne-Jones' *The Sirens*; and Jacopo Tintoretto's *Portrait of a Young Lady*.

In 1928, *Connoisseur* magazine reviewed the last two Holford volumes:

> *Volume I. Of this handsome pair appeared, shall we say felicitously, on the very eve*
> *of the Holford sale at Christie's last summer. Its function is therefore memorial*
> *rather than actual for there is no longer a Holford collection of Italian painting. On*
> *the other hand, of course, it is doubly valuable as a record of departed glories. Volume*
> *II. Still functions as the Catalogue of a Holford collection yet in being...In the*
> *Spanish school, the Velasquez* Philip IV, *when young,* the *Philip when old,*
> *presumably by Mazo, and two typically solemn Murillo portraits are*
> *conspicuous...With its two hundred illustrations and handsome mounting, this finely*
> *produced record of the Holford collection will form a treasured item on the shelves of*
> *advanced collectors and students; while its pages will doubtless be frequently*
> *consulted by historians for the valuable information they afford concerning many*
> *noteworthy works of art.[17]*

Since Ringling did own a large collection of art journals, it is plausible that he turned to them for advice on which books to purchase. "The Connoisseur Bookshelf" (from which the above review is cited) and "Books Received" were regular columns in *Connoisseur*, and *The Burlington Magazine* regularly listed and reviewed books in its "Art Books of the Month" and "Recent Art" columns.

Four years of *Christie's Season*, from 1928 to 1931, were found in offices in the Museum and Cà d'Zan. The 1928 edition reviews the Holford sale (fig. 29): "The larger version of *Philip IV*, by Velasquez (pl. 21), which was bought for 3,300 guineas by Mr. Ringling, who is proud to be styled 'The Modern Barnum,' is probably the same picture which realized only 120 guineas in the Alton Towers sale, 1857."[18]

One of the most important titles in Ringling's library for us today is the *Collection Emile Gavet: Catalogue Raisonné Précédé d'une Etude Historique et Archologique sur les Oeuvres d'Art qui*

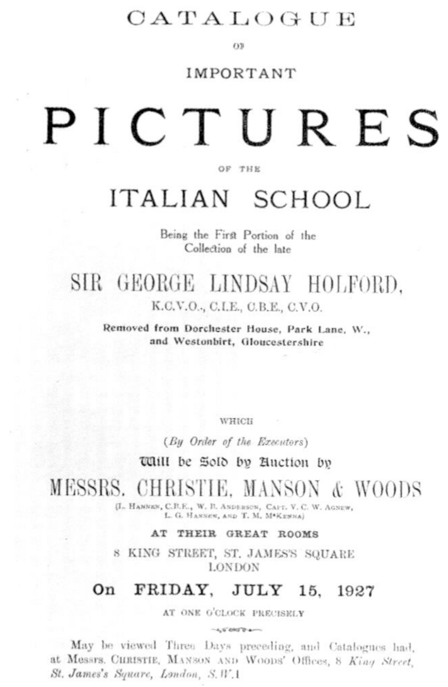

CATALOGUE

OF

IMPORTANT

PICTURES

OF THE

ITALIAN SCHOOL

Being the First Portion of the
Collection of the late

SIR GEORGE LINDSAY HOLFORD,

K.C.V.O., C.I.E., C.B.E., C.V.O.

Removed from Dorchester House, Park Lane, W.,
and Westonbirt, Gloucestershire

WHICH

(*By Order of the Executors*)

Will be Sold by Auction by

MESSRS. CHRISTIE, MANSON & WOODS

(L. HANNEN, C.B.E., W. B. ANDERSON, CAPT. V. C. W. AGNEW,
L. G. HANNEN, AND T. M. M^cKENNA)

AT THEIR GREAT ROOMS

8 KING STREET, ST. JAMES'S SQUARE
LONDON

On FRIDAY, JULY 15, 1927

AT ONE O'CLOCK PRECISELY

May be viewed Three Days preceding, and Catalogues had, at Messrs. CHRISTIE, MANSON AND WOODS' Offices, 8 *King Street, St. James's Square, London, S.W.*1

Figure 29. Title page of Ringling's copy of the 1927 Holford sale by Christie's in London. At this and the second Holford sale in the following year, Ringling bought numerous important works, including the portrait of Philip IV by Velasquez.

Composent Cette Collection, issued by the Imprimerie de D. Jouaust, Paris, in 1889 (pl. 34). Published in a limited edition of 50, the library owns two copies, numbers 37 and 38, the latter inscribed by Emile Gavet. In 1928 Ringling purchased the large Gavet collection of fine and decorative arts, including one of the Museum's finest works, Piero di Cosimo's *The Building of a Palace* (pl. 35). At the time of Ringling's death, one copy of the *Collection Emile Gavet* was among the only six books found in the Cà d'Zan living room.[19] Another major and unique purchase — of a collection of more than 2,300 objects — from 1928 is represented in the catalogue *Cypriote & Classical Antiquities: Duplicates of the Cesnola & Other Collections: Sold by Order of the Trustees of the Metropolitan Museum of Art* issued by Anderson Galleries in New York.

Another catalogue which played a significant role in the building of John Ringling's art collection was the Fonderie Aristiche Riunite's *Bronzes, Marbres, Argenterie*, of the Naples firm of J. Chiurazzi et fils. In its pages one finds photographs of bronze castings of classical sculpture with prices and three patinas available — Pompei, Herculanum and Moderne. The sculptures that Ringling ordered from Chiurazzi can be found today on the Museum grounds.

Though most of John Ringling's art books were found in his home, the McGurk inventory listed more than 65 volumes and "numerous catalogues of Art Sales and Galleries and Pamphlets, etc." from the Museum office. Three sets of biographical dictionaries of artists found there are frequently consulted in the library today: Michael Bryans' *Dictionary of Painters and Engravers*, Alfred von Wurzbach's *Niederländisches Künstler- Lexikon*, and John Denison Champlin's *Cyclopedia of Painters and Painting*. Other early imprints from the seventeenth and eighteenth centuries form the basis for a rare book collection which was later augmented with purchases by Curtis G. Coley, the Museum's third director, between 1965 and 1972.

Some art historians published, in the manner of Vasari, their own "artists' lives" complete with engraved portraits. Three such titles of major importance (all of which were exhibited at the

Ringling Museum library's 1969 exhibition), include Giovanni Pietro Bellori's *Vite de' Pittori, Scultori ed Architetti Moderni* from 1672. Bellori, a literary figure, connoisseur and former librarian for Queen Christina of Sweden, was assisted in the creation of this book by his friend, Nicholas Poussin. Bibliographer Chamberlain calls the Bellori "invaluable as a source of information on the Carracci, Caravaggio, Barocci, Domenichino, etc. Rubens' and Poussin's art included with the Italian masters."[20] Another seventeenth century title found was the two-volume 1678 edition of Carlo Cesare Malvasia's *Felsina pittrice; vite di' pittori bolognesi alla maesta christianissima di Luigi XIII* (fig. 30). Malvasia, a Bolognese nobleman and collector, is still a recognized source for the history of painting in northern Italy, and his book is a basic source for artists of Bologna. Another early treatise on the Italian schools of painting is the six-volume 1818 edition of Luigi Antonio Lanzi's *Storia pittorica della Italia dal risorgimento delle belle arti fin presso al fine del XVIII secolo.*

One of the most fascinating titles in the rare book collection originally belonging to John Ringling is a 1913 facsimile of the Gutenberg Bible (pl. 28). Johannes Gutenberg (1400-68), regarded as the European inventor of movable type printing, best known for his 42-line Bible (or Biblia Latina, c. 1455). The original Gutenberg Bible has been called "the cornerstone in the history of printing and of any collection of printed books"[21] and "the most perfectly realized of printed books. Modeled entirely from the manuscript tradition, it is a triumph of its art...a work to rival all subsequent printed books, with no compromise of craftsmanship at any stage."[22] The Ringling facsimile was published by Insel-Verlag in Leipzig and is number 287 of a limited edition of 300 copies. The colored numerals and other page decorations were taken from the original hand decorations of the copies of the Gutenberg Bible in the Royal Library in Berlin and the State Library in Fulda, and has been called the most sought-after of all facsimile editions. The Bible is even more special in that is inscribed to "Mr. John Ringling" in the year 1931 by Otto H.F. Vollbehr, a German historian and famous collector of books and incunabula (in short, any book printed between 1450 and 1500).

An exhibition of Vollbehr's collection was held in New York in 1926, the same year Vollbehr made headlines in a 1926 issue of *Art News* when he purchased one of the original Gutenberg Bibles

Figure 30. Title page of Ringling's 1678 edition of Carlo Ceasare Malvasia's *Felsina Pittrice; vite de' pittori alla maesta christianissima di Luigi XIII.*

for $275,000. Pynson Press printed a catalogue to accompany the New York show, *Vollbehr incunabula at National Arts Club of New York from 8/23 to Sept 30 MCMXXVI.* Perhaps Ringling and Vollbehr became acquainted at the time of this exhibition or at one of the many book sales held at Anderson Galleries. The details and circumstances of their relationship have yet to be discovered, but one result of it was the bestowal of the Gutenberg facsimile to Ringling. Interestingly, the facsimile — among the most valuable volumes, if not the single most valuable book, in Ringling's collection — was not listed among the other books on the McGurk inventory or a later inventory list of the John Ringling library created by the Museum librarian. However, it may be listed on the 1940 warehouse inventory from his Park Avenue residence as a two-volume "Latin (?) Manuscripts (Reprints)," in which case the preparer of the list failed to recognize the facsimile's significance.

The small number of volumes in his library inscribed to John Ringling may well indicate that he purchased most of the collection for himself. One book inscribed to the great collector is of paramount interest. *Rembrandt Paintings in America* is a large 1931 tome signed by the author, the eminent early Dutch authority Wilhelm R. Valentiner (figs. 31 and 32). This book is of special value to the Ringling Museum of Art collection as it contains reproductions of the works Ringling purchased as Rembrandts: *The Deposition (The Lamentation)* and *Portrait of a Lady* as well as the Portrait of *St. John the Evangelist Writing* (now attributed to an imitator of Rembrandt and held by the Museum of Fine Arts in Boston).

Most of the folios in the John Ringling library are of the decorative arts and architectural ornament, in addition to some splendidly colored plates of historic costumes through all the ages of man. *Le Costume historique*, a multi-volume set of 300 plates from 1876, documents with fine attention to detail the modes and manners of all periods and world locales (pl. 29). French essays describe the collection of illustrations which includes not only clothing but also period jewelry, objects

of art, vehicles, home furnishings, weapons and customs.
These oversized portfolios are in striking contrast to four
delicate, almost pocket-sized books of hand-colored
engravings of Parisian fashions, also in Ringling's library.

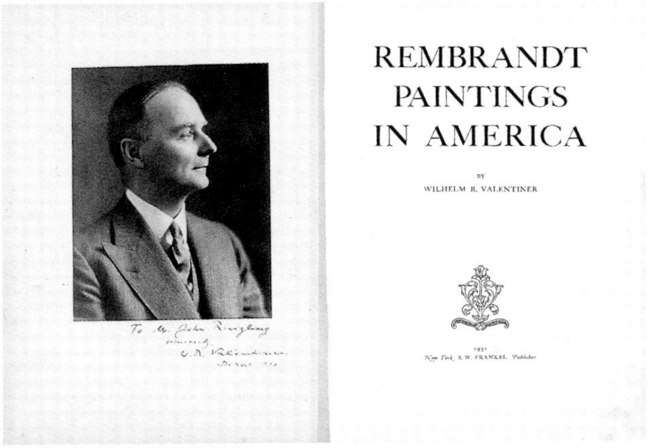

Figure 31. Fronticepiece and title page of Wilhelm R. Valentiner's 1931 *Rembrandt Paintings in America*, inscribed to Ringling. Three Ringling acquisitions are reproduced in the volume.

General texts on porcelain and Chinese jade
shared shelf space with those on decorative furniture, the
history of furniture since antiquity, and silver work by American master craftsmen. One interesting
title is Robert Wemyss Symonds' *Old English walnut & lacquer furniture: the present-day condition and
value and the methods of the furniture-faker in producing spurious pieces*, published in 1923.

Ringling had few books on sculpture, as compared with his many volumes on painting and
the decorative arts, though his interest in ancient sculpture is apparent. *The Classical Sculpture Gallery*,
a four-volume series by von Reber and Bayersdorfer published from 1897 to 1900, showcases
reproductions from the galleries, churches and private collections of Europe. Each volume is bound in
deep blue cloth accented with lettering and ornamentation in gold leaf. Ringling also owned a limited
edition copy of *The Life of Benvenuto Cellini* from 1927.

But what of the art of the hundred years preceding Ringling's death, or indeed the work of
his contemporaries? As a world traveler and avid art collector, Ringling was surely aware of current
trends in all media. His few books on modern art — on Degas, Van Gogh and Cézanne — and his
foray into Pre-Raphaelite painting seem to indicate a piqued and passing curiosity in the recent and
contemporary, if nothing more. A few unique titles found in his library, though, include Leonce
Benedite's *Rodin* with 40 plates in heliogravure; *Impressionist painting: its genesis and development*; and
Contemporary American sculpture, a catalogue from a 1929 exhibition in San Francisco. Did Ringling
perhaps visit this show?

Some volumes in the John Ringling library defy easy characterization and constitute, by their
very survival, a kind of anomaly. They range from *The Crusader: a tragedy of the middle ages in five acts*
and a tableau (on whose first page John Ringling's name is penned in script with an insignia of the
highest order of freemasonry) to the work of a highly desirable artist and naturalist, William Beebe's

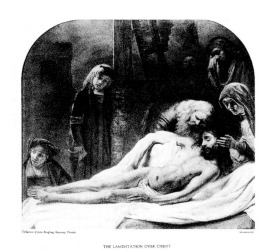

Figure 32. A full page illustration, from Valentiner's *Rembrandt Paintings in America*, of *The Lamentation* (see plate 17 for a color reproduction), purchased by Ringling in London in 1929 as a Rembrandt. While the museum did not open to the public until 1930, works from the collection were becoming known to the world through publications such as this.

rare four-volume *The Monograph of the Pheasants* (pl. 30). It is not known from whom or why Ringling purchased this natural history title, but a catalogue from Ringling's collection perhaps affords a clue. Among his many catalogues was that of a 1928 Anderson Galleries sale, *The Library of Norman James, Baltimore, Md. Natural History, Americana, Sport.* Item number 184 is an offering of the Beebe four-volume set on pheasants but there are no marks in the catalogue indicating its purchase by Ringling at this time. *The Mind of a Gorilla* bears an inscription to John Ringling from Yale professor Robert Yerkes. This 1926 psychological monograph on animal intelligence features "Miss Congo," Mable Ringling's infamous pet kept in a wooden hut near Cà d'Zan.[23]

The McGurk inventory shows that Ringling owned many volumes of literature, but unfortunately few of these left to the estate can be accounted for. One fine set that has serendipitously survived is *Ruskin's Works* in 27 volumes, probably from 1899. There is no doubting the affinity between the great circus man and this leading Victorian art critic. Venice, for Ruskin, was the "paradise of cities," and Ringling would surely have been familiar with *The Stones of Venice* and *Lectures on Art*. Ringling owned an 1897 edition of Ruskin's *Lectures on landscape: delivered at Oxford in Lent term, 1871*, and a 1925 copy of *Venice on foot: with the itinerary of the Grand Canal and several direct routes to useful places*, conjures up images of Ringling traipsing through the city and paying homage to the art of his and Mable's passion.

Reassembled together for the first time in many years and quietly evoking the spirit of a man and the dreams of a collector, the John Ringling library is a testament to his grand legacy.

The Astor Rooms

by Michael Conforti

Mrs. William Backhouse Astor was perhaps the most powerful social lioness America has ever known. With her family's social rank and the Astor's fabulous wealth, Caroline Schermerhorn Astor made late nineteenth century New York society into her personal domain and repulsed every challenge to her position as its ruling queen. Her control over admission to New York's highest social circles was enforced through the adroit manipulation of the guest lists to her famous parties. By extending or withholding the coveted invitations, Mrs. Astor was able to chastise the social misdemeanors of her friends even as she stifled the bolder encroachments of the *nouveaux riches*. Her task was made easier by the limited size of her ballroom, which could comfortably accommodate no more than four hundred guests. That "Four Hundred" — so-called by her social secretary Ward McAllister in his famous utterance — came to define New York society in the last decades of the nineteenth century.

Figure 33. Photograph of the northwest salon of the Astor residence at 840 Fifth Avenue in New York City, circa 1907. In the corner at center is a full length oil portrait of Caroline Schermerhorn Astor by Emile Auguste Carolus-Duran, now in the Metropolitan Museum of Art.

Mrs. Astor's ballroom was situated in her brownstone at Fifth Avenue and 34th Street, where she had lived with her husband since their 1859 marriage. But in the early 1890s, with her only son, John Jacob Astor IV, planning to marry and her nephew, William Waldorf Astor, building a hotel next door, she decided to relocate. She resolved to move uptown, as many of her friends had already done, and the old 34th Street house was subsequently demolished to make room for the hotel addition that would become the first Waldorf-Astoria. She commissioned Richard Morris Hunt, then the most prominent of New York's residential architects, to build her a new double house at Fifth Avenue and 65th Street. She would live in one half, while John Jacob IV and his family would occupy the other (fig. 34).

The exterior of the new Astor residence was conceived in the French Renaissance style

Figure 34. Partial view of the exterior of the Astor residence, looking northeast from the park side of Fifth Avenue, circa 1890s. The southwest cream salon, now gallery 19, occupied the southwest corner of the first floor of the double mansion, with windows overlooking both Fifth Avenue and 65th Street. The windows of the adjoining library, now gallery 20, are further to the right, out of view.

popularized by Hunt. Incorporating Mansard roofs and turreted dormers, the house suggested a sixteenth century French château adapted to life in late nineteenth century America. Like Hunt's other houses of the 1890s, the Astor mansion was filled with paneled period rooms commissioned from Jules Allard and Company of Paris and New York. The Allard firm specialized in recreating French interiors for moneyed Americans eager to link themselves with the elegance, grandeur and refinement associated with certain historical periods.

The Astor mansion, however, stood no more than thirty years. In the mid-1920s, Vincent Astor decided to tear down his father's and grandmother's house, and at his direction the contents and works of art were sold at auction in 1926.[1] John Ringling, then planning his Sarasota museum, purchased two rooms: the salon, or main reception room, and the adjoining dining room/library from John Jacob IV's half of the double house. The original decoration of the salon, replete with painted over-door panels and elaborate gilt moldings, incorporated predominantly Louis XV or Rococo style elements that recall the interior of a mid-century Parisian *hôtel particulier* (figs. 35, 36 and 37). The adjoining dining room — later converted to a library — was finished in carved oak and parcel gilding that loosely followed Louis XIV precedents in interior design (figs. 38, 39 and 40). The large panels of this room once framed tapestries, as was popular in late nineteenth century residences. Ringling replaced them with early eighteenth century Dutch paintings.

The two Astor rooms acquired by Ringling do not strictly observe French precedent. Rather, they are amalgamations created by Hunt and Allard that incorporate elements from numerous eighteenth century French interior styles. Strapwork motifs, such as those on the dining room pilasters, follow early eighteenth century models, while the roundels and swags above the doors were more common in the late eighteenth century. Also, late nineteenth century New York houses required doorways far wider than any to be seen in eighteenth century French domestic interiors. In numerous decorative details, however, both rooms are consistent with French precursors.

The two Astor rooms in the Ringling Museum are among the few examples of late nineteenth century French style interior decoration preserved in American museums. As such, they represent a fascinating tradition in which interiors functioned as subtle cultural symbols as well as sites for social ritual. The nineteenth and early twentieth century American predilection for rooms evoking the luxury of European pasts or the romance of exotic cultures reflected nuanced social codes through which a patron communicated his values and historical interests to his contemporaries. Whether the chosen style was Louis XIV or Elizabethan, Moorish or Japanese, each choice connoted a desire to identify with the social, political and intellectual values associated with that historical period or culture.

The eighteenth century French interior was first revived by the British Whig aristocracy in the period immediately following the defeat of Napoleon and the restoration of the Bourbon monarchy in France.[2] Identification with *ancien régime* values represented a reaction to radical political reforms proposed in England in the 1820s, and the choice of this interior style was seen by contemporaries as reinforcing the values of monarchy as expressed by the most absolute of earlier sovereigns, Louis XIV. In the early years of the Second Empire, members of the French *haute bourgeoisie* eagerly embraced the eighteenth century style for their domestic residences, with the Empress Eugénie setting the tone for nostalgic identification by entertaining in authentic eighteenth century rooms while wearing the clothes of the famous guillotined queen, Marie Antoinette.[3]

The popularity of the French interior grew in the last decades of the nineteenth century both in Europe and America. By the time Caroline Astor commissioned Hunt to design and build a new double house in New York, the French style had come to symbolize the supreme standard of cultural refinement and sophistication for America's rich, associating them with the intellect and culture of this most respected of historical periods.[4] Houses and their interiors came to be seen as backdrops for cultured lives, and those lives often included identification with specific historical figures through costumed play acting. In an era when Empress Eugénie dressed as Marie Antoinette and received Queen Victoria with flawless eighteenth century protocol, at a time when Ludwig II of Bavaria staged

Figure 35. Photograph of the furnished southwest cream salon, circa 1910 shortly after the completion, by Carrère and Hastings, of the conversion of the double mansion to single family usage for John Jacob Astor IV. Photo: The Architectural Record.

Figure 36. Photograph of the southwest salon, shortly before the sale and subsequent demolition of the house by Vincent Astor in 1926. Note the hardwood floor in herring-bone pattern, the ceiling and overdoor paintings and gilding on the coved ceiling. Note also that electric wall sconces have been changed since 1910.

Figure 37. The Astor salon as it appeared in the Ringling Museum, before the 1990 renovation. The wall paneling is original, while the coved ceiling was recreated in plaster by Claude Baylor, a craftsman from Sarasota. The room was given an oak floor, and mirrors were installed in place of the overdoor paintings. The marble fireplace is not original to the Astor room.

Figure 38. The library in 1910, just after its conversion from a dining room by Carrère and Hastings for John Jacob Astor IV. Note the absence of a large chandelier that originally hung from the ceiling center. Note also the tapestry hung in the large wall panel and the oil portrait of John Jacob in the overmantle. Ringling did not purchase the tapestry or the marble fireplace. Photo: The Architectural Record.

Figure 39. The library in 1926, at the time of the Astor sale. In 1913, an allegorical ceiling painting by James Wall Finn had been added. The painting was acquired along with the oak and parcel gilt paneling by John Ringling at the 1926 sale.

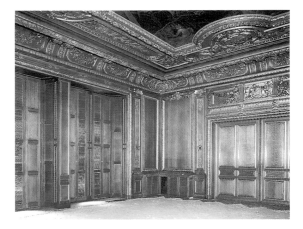

Figure 40. The southwest corner of the library in 1926, showing, at left, the shuttered windows overlooking 65th Street and, at right, the sliding pocket doors communicating with the cream salon. The pocket doors were finished in oak on the library side and *Laqué* cream on the salon side. In the Ringling Museum in Sarasota, John H. Phillips replicated the exact southern exposure the two rooms had in New York City.

conversations with Louis XIV in his neo-Rococo German Castles, Caroline Astor had herself painted and often appeared at balls in the guise of Mary, Queen of Scots. In this era of historical recreation expressed in both houses and costumed dress, Mrs. Astor's architect enhanced his professional image by having himself photographed in the guise of the thirteenth century Italian artist Giovanni Cimabue.[5]

The architect Richard Morris Hunt was much in demand in the second half of the nineteenth century. Having spent twelve years in France, studying at the École des Beaux Arts and working as an assistant in the Paris office of Hector Martin Lefuel, Hunt was superbly trained and the most educated and historically sophisticated architect America had yet produced. The house he built in 1882 for Mr. and Mrs. William K. Vanderbilt at Fifth Avenue and 52nd Street was a stunning model of sixteenth century French architecture successfully adapted to an urban American setting. It solidified Hunt's reputation as the designer best equipped to express America's historical longings in architecture. Its interiors, representing a variety of early styles, were articulated largely in carved stone and wood employing far less upholstery and ornamental patterning than was typical at that time.[6] A triumph for the savvy and ambitious Alva Vanderbilt, the house was formally opened with an inaugural party so eagerly anticipated in society circles that even Caroline Astor temporarily suspended her snubs of the upstart Vanderbilts in order to secure an invitation for her daughter.

Marble House, Hunt's next commission for Alva Vanderbilt, was realized in Louis XIV style and had the most expensive interior created in America in the late nineteenth century (fig. 41). Finished in 1892, this Newport, Rhode Island, mansion featured a marble lined dining room inspired by the Salon d'Hercule at Versailles and a gilded reception room augmenting allusions to the Galerie des Glaces at Versailles with carved details copied from Duban's 1850-51 renovations to the Galerie d'Apollon at the Louvre. Here, Hunt and Alva Vanderbilt achieved a unity of historical reference unprecedented in any other American house built up to that time. In a clear allusion to the monarch emulated in the interiors, a copy of Bernini's bust of Louis XIV, executed by Edmé Suchetet, was even installed on the main stairway landing. And as a spectacular homage to the man who conceived the setting, Mrs. Vanderbilt flanked the Sun King with relief portraits, by Karl Bitter, of Hunt and his seventeenth century mentor, François Mansart.[7]

In Hunt's interiors of the 1890s, the eighteenth century French style came to supersede all others. Only Biltmore, the extraordinary North Carolina estate he created for George W. Vanderbilt, maintained the French renaissance idiom for the principal reception room and the exterior. At Ochre Court, for example, the Newport house Hunt built for Ogden Goelet as he

Figure 41. The entrance façade of Marble House, in Newport, Rhode Island, designed by Richard Morris Hunt for Alva Vanderbilt. The Vanderbilts acquired the Emile Gavet collection, subsequently purchased by John Ringling. Gavet's collection was installed in a specially designed Gothic room at Marble House, illustrated in figs. 49, 50. Photograph: Courtesy of Rhode Island Historical Society.

was working on Marble House, nearly every downstairs receiving room, as well as every bedroom, was executed in an eighteenth century French style. This marked the beginning of the dominance of French art and culture in American architecture and interior design, a dominance that would be summarized in the highly influential book by Ogden Codman and Edith Wharton, *The Decoration of Houses*, first published in 1897. In their collaborative study, the young and ambitious architect Codman and the soon to be famous novelist argued that the French interior was not merely one among many periods and styles available for historical quotation, but was *the* style supreme over all others, the historical reference that connoted "Culture" itself. The superiority of *le goût dix-huitième* continued well into the twentieth century throughout the United States.

Hunt summered in Newport, and his nearness to its New York-based summer colony resulted in many commissions for houses. In 1890, as Marble House and Ochre Court were under construction, Mrs. Caroline Astor asked Hunt to help her remodel "Beechwood." This Astor cottage built in an Italianate style in the 1860s, was virtually next door to Marble House. The commission included the addition of two mid-eighteenth century style French interiors — one a large rococo revival ballroom, still extant, with a vast expanse of glazed double doors opening onto a majestic Atlantic view. In the following summer Hunt began discussions with Mrs. Astor and her son toward the design of a new two-family townhouse in New York. The firm began to draw up plans in the autumn of 1891.

The year and a half in which the plans for the new Astor house were discussed and refined were a period of great personal difficulty for Caroline Astor. While assisting her only son through his wedding, she was forced to endure relentless gossiping in the press about her rivalry with her garrulous nephew, William Waldorf Astor. It was reported that William Waldorf wanted to depose his aunt from her position as female head of the Astor family and install his own wife in her place.[8] The press had also learned that one of Mrs. Astor's four married daughters had run off to Europe with a New Jersey neighbor. In an attempt to settle the scandal, William Backhouse Astor had followed them across the Atlantic. In April, 1892, he suffered a heart attack in Paris and died.

The pressure of these events weighed on Mrs. Astor, along with her son's need for separate quarters and her nephew's decision to begin construction on his new hotel next door to her 34th Street townhouse. Originally, she and Hunt discussed two houses on separate Fifth Avenue sites. One of Hunt's presentation drawings for Mrs. Astor's house depicted a majestically detailed French Renaissance château that would have rivaled the late medieval mansion Hunt was then building for Elbridge Gerry.[9] She vetoed the design, however, and, now a widow, chose the more modest and practical option of combining her own and her son's residences on two 50 by 100 foot lots at 840 and 842 Fifth Avenue. The final plans for a massive double house with a common principal entrance and elaborate exterior detailing balanced a sense of practicality with the grandeur expected of clients as prominent as the Astors. The main reception rooms were realized in the eighteenth century French style favored by Hunt's clients. Costing $1.5 million to build and $750,000 to furnish, the Astor double house represented a certain restraint in an upper bracket tradition of architectural and decorative excess. It was widely reported at the time that Marble House had cost an amazing $9 million, making it by far the most expensive house created in America in the late nineteenth century.

The new Astor mansion was inaugurated in a series of social events in February, 1896. Guests arrived through a principal carriage entrance situated on Fifth Avenue. Alighting under a *porte-cochère*, visitors passed into a foyer which presented two doors — to the left, Mrs. Astor's, and to the right, her son's. Both doorways led to a large two-story hall, widow's and son's identical halves divided by a wall with doors that could be opened for large parties. In the central interior court of each house, Hunt maintained the flavor of the exterior architecture, here articulated with mannerist style figural sculpture by Karl Bitter (fig. 42). Proceeding east past the grand staircase, one reached the ballroom and art gallery common to both houses, executed in a grandiloquent, if by then somewhat dated, French Second Empire style (figs. 43 and 44, pls. 32 and 33).

Adjacent to the entrance of Mrs. Astor's wing was a small rococo reception room installed with Louis XVI style furniture. Beyond was the principal reception room, the detailing of which loosely followed early Louis XV precedents. There, a feeling of spaciousness was created by means of three arched mirror bays. A dark oak early Louis XIV style dining room, maintaining the traditional Victorian desire to dine in unpainted paneled rooms, followed rooms which in the past had utilized Elizabethan or Jacobean vocabularies.

John Jacob's house paralleled his mother's both in plan and in the integration of the French interior style throughout the downstairs receiving rooms. The two wings differed in detail, however. The son's principal reception room — now in the Ringling Museum — was both the most ornate and historically correct in the double house. Well lit by large windows opening on both Fifth Avenue and 65th Street, the room had no need to incorporate the expansive mirrors that, on his mother's side, had somewhat undermined its historical accuracy. The carved decorative detailing in the room strictly followed eighteenth century French precedents. The enormous width of the doorway leading to the dining room was the room's boldest concession to contemporary taste. In conformity to late nineteenth century practice as well, a vast array of reproduction objects — from screens to chairs to Chinese vases— filled the interior.

Certain peculiarities of Hunt's design — the single entrance to the two wings, the removable wall of the central hall, and the double entrance to the single ballroom — appear to have anticipated the eventual conversion of the double house to a single family residence. After Caroline Astor died in 1908, John Jacob immediately commissioned the prominent New York architectural firm Carrère and Hastings to alter the house for single family use. The remodeling was dramatic. The entire central stairway was removed, creating one large court that brought the house nearer to the sparer, and in this case more Italianate, decoration favored in the early twentieth century.[10] Mrs. Astor's dining room

Figure 42. View from the foyer east into the inner hall and staircase of Caroline Astor's side of the Fifth Avenue double mansion. Under the staircase is the entrance to the art gallery-ballroom that accomodated 1,200— three times the capacity of that in her old brownstone at 34th and Fifth Avenue.

Figure 44. View west from inside the art gallery-ballroom, circa 1907, looking toward the double doors that opened on the respective inner halls of the double mansion's two separate residences.

Figure 43. View east into the art gallery-ballroom, circa 1907. Note, to lower left of chimneypiece, Jean-Baptiste Eduard Detaille's *The Retreat* (pl. 32) and, on the lower right, Ferdinand Roybet's *The Connoisseurs* (pl. 33), two paintings acquired by John Ringling at the 1926 sale.

was updated in a classical style to serve her son's family, and John Jacob's old dining room — now in the Ringling — was converted to a library. While no photos of the dining room before its conversion have survived, its present natural wood finish was probably original.[11] The classical detailing of its Louis XIV style as well as its natural finish made it a logical clubman's reading room.

John Jacob Astor IV perished when the ill-fated S.S. Titanic struck an iceberg and went down on its maiden voyage in 1912, just two years after the conversion of the house was completed. His second wife lived there until 1919, when Vincent Astor, John Jacob's son by first marriage, moved in with his wife.[12] They stayed until 1925, when the decision was made to sell the house for $3.5 million as the site for the future Temple Emmanu-El. The two rooms John Ringling purchased at the widely publicized and closely watched 1926 auction were the two finest remaining in the house.[13]

John Ringling preserved the two Astor rooms for his museum in Sarasota just 30 years after their original commission and installation by Hunt and Jules Allard and Company. The Astor house was only one of many luxurious New York dwellings destroyed as the city expanded, and these rooms are among a handful that have survived intact. Traditional historical preservation, however, was probably not Mr. Ringling's primary concern in making this purchase. Instead, he was responding, in his own iconoclastic and impresario manner, to two factors much influencing interior design and museum installation in the early twentieth century: a heightened interest in contextual installations that gave rise to period rooms in every major museum at the time, and a Francophilia finding expression in all aspects of elite life, but particularly in the field of interior decoration.

John Ringling would not build a French château. He had in mind something more appropriate to Florida history and climate, a Mediterranean, in fact a Venetian house with an Italian Renaissance-style museum attached to it. The recreated Italian or Spanish villa had come to be favored by Americans building estates in warmer regions. James Deering's Vizcaya, in Miami, Addison Mizner's first houses in Palm Beach, and William Randolph Hearst's San Simeon in California were all built between 1910 and the 1930s.

In personality, Ringling was close to Hearst in worldly ambition and collecting eclecticism. Each was a showman seeking to monumentalize his success through architecture, as practiced in the early twentieth century. While Hearst chose a Spanish, ecclesiastical- style structure for his house and surrounded it with lavish gardens overlooking the Pacific, Ringling fixed on the fanciful recreation of a grand Venetian palazzo on the Florida coast. His desire for the theatrical effect of large-scale period environments motivated his purchase of the French eighteenth century style Astor rooms for his neo-Renaissance Sarasota museum. But as the two rooms are among the few New York period interiors from the era to survive in an art museum context, one could say that Ringling's desire for effect did not lack a certain foresight.

Mr. Conforti wishes to thank Gene Ray for this edited adaptation of two lectures delivered at the Ringling Museum in 1984 and 1994 and Ann Friedman for her assistance with the initial research for this essay.
This essay and accompanying captions incorporate substantial additional research, findings and interpretation carried out by the editors and members of the Ringling curatorial staff during the final preparation of this text.

probably dead by 1907,[4] the fame of his collection lived on in the sale rooms.

The history of the purchase and installation of the Gavet objects in the Gothic Room documents a very American phenomenon. The interest in French decorative arts, largely from the eighteenth century but also from late Medieval and Renaissance periods, grew steadily over the course of the nineteenth century. The Gothic Room (figs. 49 and 50) — based on the house of Jacques Coeur at Bourges, which one of Hunt's associates might have seen while travelling in France in the 1880s — was a product of the rise of the American leisure class, the members of which looked directly to the aristocratic styles of European nobility in the creation of their palaces. The demand for interior decoration on a grand scale in the last decades of the nineteenth century led to the creation of a new category of merchant-craftsmen such as Allard, who opened a New York office in 1885.[5]

Allard's first New York commission was the boudoir for Alva at 660 Fifth Avenue, which he got from Christian Herter, complete with a ceiling painting by the Parisian artist Jules Lefebvre.[6] The taste for period furnishings and decoration coincided with the destruction of many seventeenth and eighteenth century hôtels in Paris during the construction of Baron Haussmann's Grands Boulevards, and some of these interiors made their way into American residences. When the real thing was not available or desirable, traditional craftsmen were called in to replicate it. Many period interiors eventually found their way to the decorative arts collections of American museums, where they have been, in many cases, reconstituted frankly as period rooms that document prevailing taste of the period in which they were recreated.[7]

The relationship between dealers, decorators, collectors and patrons was highly controlled, often negotiated by the dealers to maximize influence. A passage from a letter that Henry Duveen sent from Paris to his brother Joseph in New York in 1913 gives an idea of the nature of this relationship: "I cabled you from Montecarlo that the decoration of important houses of our clients must be kept entirely under our direction, that is to say, if we introduce Allom or Carlhian to our clients who are having work done, any interviews which take place between the client and the Decorator should be held in our presence...Perhaps it would be well to discuss sometimes for the mere sake of discussion, and with a view to showing our client that we are master and that we know our

Figure 45. Illustration from the 1889 catalogue raisonné
The Emile Gavet collection displayed in his Paris apartment.

Figure 46. Illustration from the 1889 catalogue raisonné
The Emile Gavet collection displayed in his Paris apartment.

Figure 47. Illustration from the 1889 catalogue raisonné
The Emile Gavet collection displayed in his Paris apartment.

Figure 48. Illustration from the 1889 catalogue raisonné
The Emile Gavet collection displayed in his Paris apartment.

business. We do not want it to appear as if the Decorator is in any way the master, and we should always keep the whip-hand..." This passage indicates the extent to which the process of purchase and decoration of houses was a collaborative effort between various interest groups.[8]

Molinier, in his suggestion that the Gavet collection represented the furnishings of a palace, could not have addressed more directly the aspirations of Alva Erskine Smith Vanderbilt, who was beginning construction on her "cottage" in Newport that very year. For its architect, Alva had engaged Richard Morris Hunt, with whom she had worked closely on the design and construction of her New York townhouse at 660 Fifth Avenue. Alva had made sure that her husband, William Kissam Vanderbilt, had placed the property under her name. Notations on drawings in the Hunt archives in Washington testify to her direct involvement in all stages of design and construction.[9] The construction itself was elaborate, and an entire wharf had to be leased to unload the shipments of marble arriving from as far away as Italy and Algiers. Alva had a tall wooden fence constructed around the site as the building progressed and kept watch with dogs lest a curious neighbor attempt to scale the wall. The mansion was revealed in August of 1892 at a gala housewarming party. The opulence of Marble House was celebrated immediately, and prints of it were circulated around the nation. Cleveland Amory called Marble House "the climax of the American Dream."[10]

It is tempting to see John Ringling's aspirations in building his seaside palace, Cà d'Zan, some twenty years later, as parallel to the creation of great Newport mansions of the 1890s. Ringling probably bought much of the Gavet collection from Alva's Gothic Room in 1928. Sources are vague about how parts of Mrs. Belmont's collection were made available to Ringling, but the most likely hypothesis is that Julius Böhler, who served as Ringling's adviser and brokered many of his purchases, was involved.[11] It has also been suggested that Joseph Duveen played a role, but there is no conclusive evidence in this regard. It is significant that Ringling also bought large sections of wood paneling from the Astor mansion on Fifth Avenue. This episode is parallel to his purchase of the Gavet objects and is discussed by Michael Conforti in his contribution to this volume. Perhaps it was his intention to recreate not only the palace of the Renaissance, but an Astor or Vanderbilt palace of the gay 90s, the last glimmers of which were about to be dashed by the stock market crash of 1929.

When John Ringling arranged to purchase a large number of objects from the Gavet collection from Alva Vanderbilt Belmont in 1928, he was probably buying their provenance as much as the objects themselves. In other purchases, Ringling had demonstrated his admiration for the splendid interiors of great houses of New York, so the opportunity presented by the availability of the Gavet collection was certainly not lost on him. When the Gavet objects arrived in Florida, there was no special room built for them, but Ringling displayed many of them in the Cortile of Cà d'Zan, as a period photograph documents.[12] He was no doubt attempting to create echoes of the elegance and opulence of Gavet's home in Paris, as well as that of Alva Vanderbilt's Marble House.

The Gavet collection contained a wide range of objects, both secular and religious, in a variety of media. It is not known how Ringling made the selection of objects which he purchased, but it is likely that a dealer or adviser, probably Böhler, intervened. There is no record of Ringling's visiting Marble House — where the objects presumably remained between the time Alva closed Marble House and moved to Paris and the year of the sale — so it is unlikely that Ringling viewed them *in situ*. He did presumably see the 1889 catalogue, mentioned above, a copy of which the Museum owns. This catalogue contains several photographs of the collection installed in Gavet's home in Paris. But there are no sales catalogues or receipts in the archives of the Ringling Museum. A single document, a shipping list of the collection dated December 7, 1928, which arrived in Sarasota by rail in 21 cases, is the only record of the collection's arrival in Florida.

Among the most beautiful objects that Ringling acquired from Marble House are several paintings, antique and Renaissance gems and cameos, a splendid reliquary bust of a female saint, and examples of majolica, tin-glazed earthenware from Spain and Italy. Many of the wooden sculptures and tableaux-vivants were acquired along with their supports, usually gilded and ornamented wooden shelves or brackets which created a period context and were probably made by Gavet or Allard to unify the collection in its presentation. Many of these shelves are preserved in the storage areas of the Ringling Museum and will be re-united with objects in future installations.

Perhaps the most important Renaissance painting at the Museum hung at one time in the Gothic Room at Newport, as a photograph in the Newport Historical Society shows. Piero di

Figure 49. View of the Gothic Room of Marble House, specially designed by an associate of Richard Morris Hunt for Alva Vanderbilt to house the Emile Gavet collection. Note: Piero di Cosimo's *The Building of a Palace* (pl. 35) at top center of wall. Photograph: Courtesty of Rhode Island Historical Society.

Figure 50. The Gothic Room of Marble House. Photograph: Courtesy of Rhode Island Historical Society.

Cosimo's panel depicting the building of a palace (pl. 35) was first documented in the nineteenth century in Russia, then sold to a French dealer as a Luca Signorelli and then to Gavet in 1884.[13] Piero di Cosimo, a painter active in Florence and Rome in the decades around the turn of the sixteenth century, was involved in the design of ephemeral architecture for pageants and festivals as well as in more permanent commissions. The foreground of the panel is filled with all manner of architectural activity, from the hewing of large stone blocks to the sawing of wooden beams to the intricate carving of ornamental moldings. The workers are dressed in fifteenth century clothing, suggesting that this may be an idealized portrayal of the type of monumental building projects sponsored by the Medici in and around Florence in the late fifteenth century. It is tempting to see this work's presence both in the Gavet-Vanderbilt-Belmont collection and later in the Ringling as an expression of the owners' desire to build monumental palaces. Both Marble House, where the painting hung between 1892 and 1928, and the Ringling Museum, where the painting is now located, fulfilled similar aspirations of their builders.

The female reliquary bust (pl. 36) can be seen clearly displayed between two monstrances in a cabinet in one of the photographs of the Gothic Room in Marble House. Fashioned of repouss and copper, and gilded in areas to indicate hair and clothing, the bust is encrusted with semi-precious gems, such as the heart-shaped cabochon of rose-quartz at her breast, and with colored glass. Her face was originally painted in tempera to simulate flesh, increasing the visceral qualities of the sculpture. The top of her head opens on a hinge to reveal a hollow cavity which would have housed the relic, perhaps a piece of the saint's skull. This type of reliquary is typical of French or Flemish workshops of the fifteenth century, but reliquaries which mimicked the part of the body which they held were popular all over Western Europe in the late Middle Ages. The specific identity of the saint has not been determined.

Also part of the Gavet collection was a large majolica charger, lustered in gold (pl. 37). Tin-glazed earthenware was produced in large quantities all over the Mediterranean from the fourteenth century, and by the early sixteenth century, when this plate was made, the Italian workshops in Umbria and the Marches had overtaken the Spanish centers of production in Manises and on the island of Mallorca (from where the term majolica is derived). This charger is probably from Pesaro or Deruta, both of which had flourishing potteries. It depicts a woman in three-quarter view, luxuriously dressed and bedecked in ribbons and jewels. A banderole swirls beside her, inscribed with the words, "Agniolina Bella," or Beautiful Agniolina. This type of imagery was common on plates called "coppe d'amore," or love dishes, which were probably presented as tokens of affection to the subject on the occasion of a betrothal or marriage.

Ringling also purchased several pharmacy jars, or *albarelli*, from the Gavet-Vanderbilt collection (pl. 38). These were made in Manises in the late fifteenth century and are decorated in an all-over pattern called hispano-moresque which typifies the confluence of cultures in the world of the Mediterranean. These jars were common household objects and were made to store herbs or ointments. Earthenware was practical and relatively inexpensive, and each jar could be sealed by tying a string around a piece of greased paper or fabric stretched over the mouth.

Gavet collected works of great beauty and rarity, such as the Piero di Cosimo, as well as more common examples of everyday objects such as the *albarelli* or coppe d'amore. It was this eclecticism which Alva Vanderbilt Belmont attempted to preserve in her selection and installation of objects from the Gavet collection in the Gothic Room of her Newport mansion, and which John Ringling in turn wanted to capture in his purchase of a similar range of objects for his nascent museum in Sarasota. The span of time between Gavet's sale of his collection to Alva Vanderbilt in 1889, and John Ringling's purchase from Marble House in 1928-9, brackets a distinct period in the social history of collecting in America, one which saw the transition from the glorification of European styles by a self-fashioned American aristocracy to the institutionalization of these refined tastes within the walls of the public museum.

Endnotes

The Dream Realized:
The Building of the Museum

1 William E. Suida, Memorandum, n.d. (1941?) Ringling Museum of Art (henceforth RMA) Archives.
2 *Sarasota Herald*, June 19, 1928,p.1.
3 *New York Times*, April 22, 1926, p. 10.
4 Charter of the John and Mable Ringling Museum of Art, June 16, 1927, RMA Archives.
5 Conversation with Henry Ringling North, November 18, 1986.
6 Julius W. Böhler to John H. Phillips, September 23, 1927, RMA Archives.
7 John Ringling to Julius Böhler, Telegram, July 12, 1929.
8 *The News*, Sarasota, October 7, 1956, p. 2.
9 John Ringling to Julius Böhler, Telegram, March 5, 1931, RMA Archives.
10 Inventory attached to Rembrandt Corporation minutes, Florida State Archives.
11 *Sarasota Herald*, October 4, 1931, p. 2.
12 In an *Art News* interview, Ringling named a panel of directors for the Museum, yet he never appointed any: Albert Keller, Henry Walters, Landgon Douglas, August L. Mayer, Max J. Freidlander, Sir Joseph Duveen, Baron von Hadeln. *Art News* 26 (May 5, 1928): p. 2.
13 Stock Transfer Record, July 25, 1932 Rembrandt Corporation. Ringling Estate Subject files, Florida State Archives.
14 John Ringling to Julius Böhler, October 23, 1933; Böhler to Ringling, November 11, 1933, RMA Archives.

Early Perceptions of the Museum:
A Worldview

1 *Art News*, February 25, 1928, pp. 1, 14, 15.
2 *Art News*, May 5, 1928, p. 1.
3 *TIME*, April 6, 1925, p. 15.
4 "Developing a Regional Type: With Particular Reference to the Work in Florida of Dwight James Baum," *American Architect*, August 20, 1926; "A Venetian Palace in Florida," *Country Life*, October 1927.
5 David C. Weeks, *Ringling: The Florida Years, 1911-1936*, (Gainesville: University of Florida Press, 1993), p. 185.
6 *New York Times*, April 22, 1926, p. 10.
7 *New York Times*, December 6, 1925, Section 9, pp. 3, 10.
8 Weeks, pp. 177-79.
9 *New York Times*, Feb. 4, 1927, pp. 1, 10.
10 *Art News,* May 5, 1928, p. 1; *Christian Science Monitor*, June 14, 1928; *Art Digest,* July 1928, p. 2; *American Magazine of Art*, May 1928, p. 284. *Art Digest*, calling Ringling "a singularly silent person," quoted heavily from an interview with Ringling in the *Christian Science Monitor*, and the *American Magazine of Art* in a brief article summed up the news as a "bolt out of a clear sky."
11 *Art News*, May 5, 1928, p. 1.
12 *Christian Science Monitor*, June 14, 1928. Quoted in Weeks, p. 181.
13 Weeks, p. 182.
14 *New York Times*, February 8,1929.
15 *Evening World*, March 11, 1930.
16 "Ringling Buys A Rubens," *New York Times*, October 15, 1930, p. 11; "Ringling Buys A Rubens," *Art Digest*, October 15, 1930; "Ringling's Rubens," *Art Digest*, November 1,

1930, p. 8: "Rubens' Painting of 'Pausias and Glycera' Added to the Ringling Museum," *International Studio*, January 1931, pp. 44-45.
17 *New York World*, March 16, 1930.
18 *Sarasota Herald*, February 17, 1927.
19 *Art in America*, October 1927.
20 *Burlington Magazine*, January 1928, pp. 20-21.
21 *International Studio*, November 1929, pp. 36-37.
22 Julius Böhler, "Ringling— Collector and Builder," in Weeks, p. 182.
23 *Christian Science Monitor*, June 14, 1928. Quoted in Weeks, p. 181.
24 *American Magazine of Art*, May 1928, p. 284.
25 *American Architect*, September 1931, p. 70.
26 *Art Digest*, July 1, 1931, p. 32.
27 "Arts Gain in Year in Spite of Slump," *New York Times*, January 14, 1933, p. 15.
28 "Now the Museum Pursues Learners," *New York Times*, July 3, 1932, Section 9, p. 8.
29 In contrast, when the Ringling Museum came under state ownership in the late 1940s, William Suida, the renowned art historian hired to complete a professional catalogue of the museum, also undertook the publicity efforts that were lacking during the 1930s. He published numerous articles in art journals, promoting the collection, highlighting specific paintings, and publishing new attributions.
30 Weeks, p. 180.
31 *Art Digest*, March 15, 1931.
32 Kimball, "Display Collection of the Art of the Middle Ages," *Pennsylvania Museum Bulletin* 26, (April 1931), p. 3. In *Medieval Art in America: Patterns of Collecting, 1800-*

1940, p. 138.

33 *Architectural Forum*, June 1932, p. 611.

34 *New York Times*, April 13, 1930, Section 7, p. 2.

35 Local newspapers recounted the event. Weeks, p. 210.

36 *TIME*, October 12, 1931, p. 21.

37 *New York Times*, December 20, 1930, p. 14.

38 Sarasota County Archives, Clippings Files: Ringling.

39 *New York Times*, July 28, 1933, p. 18.

40 Sarasota County Archives, Clippings File: Ringling.

41 *New York Times*, July 13, 1932, p. 3.

42 *Architectural Forum*, June 1932, pp. 561-62.

43 W.R. Valentiner, "New Additions to Works of Frans Hals." *Art in America*, June 1935, pp. 85-86.

44 *Museum News*, March 15, 1931, p. 2.

45 *Museum News*, December 15, 1936, p. 3.

46 *New York Times*, December 3, 1936.

John and Lulu: The Newly Discovered Correspondence

1 See David C. Weeks, *Ringling, The Florida Years, 1911-1936*, (Gainesville, Florida: University Press of Florida, 1993), pp. 170, 176, 199.

2 Julius W. Böhler, "John Ringling Builder and Collector," in *The Art Museum John Ringling Built*, (Sarasota, 1948), p.13 and ff.

3 Weeks, 1993, p.180.

4 Unpublished report by Böhler, ms. in Museum archives.

5 Undated letter and response.

6 Most of the paintings included in these invoices can be identified with works still in the Museum that are now catalogued according to SN numbers, indicating both the state of Florida number and that assigned in Suida's 1949 catalogue divided by schools. The identifications are as follows: Snyders - SN 234; Palma Giovane SN 95; Giampetrino SN 40, Rembrandt SN could be either SN 184 or 185; the first Murillo is probably the *Assumption* SN 350; Veronese *Portrait Group* SN 83?; *Immaculate Conception* SN 348; Fra Bartolomeo now Albertinelli SN 26; Rubens SN 224; Tintoretto SN 80?; two Bassanos SN 92-93; Luini SN 37; Stevens SN 438; Bassano *Portrait* SN 91; School of Raphael SN 595; Tintoretto *Samson and Delilah* SN 75.

7 Invoices dated 3/14/27, 4/28/27, 5/20/27, 6/27 (without a day given), and 8/5/27. The works referred to can be identified as Hals SN 251, Mainardi SN 20; Cranach SN 308; Titian SN 61, Israels SN 454; Pesnes SN 377; Caravaggio SN 109; Canos SN 344-345.

8 Cables of 10/21 and 10/29/27. The paintings mentioned the two Carraccis now Fiasellas SN 112 and 113; Pordenone SN 66; Maganza SN 101; and Dolci SN 36 or 37.

9 5/18/27 and 1/11/28. Licinio SN 68; Raeburn SN 395; Veronese SN 82.

10 Statements of 10/26 and 10/28/28. The new paintings mentioned are the Post SN 275 and Cotignola SN 49.

11 Nightletter of 1/10/29. The Frederic Spitzer collection was sold at the Anderson Galleries, New York, January 9-12, 1929. The Boucher school work (SN 376) was lot. no.529.

12 Letter of 3/13/29. The Metropolitan Museum of Art's sale on February 7, 1929 took place at the American Art Association in New York, in addition to the works sold as after Ter Borch, attributed to Bordone, and the Hans Makart (lot nos. 90, 92, 115) he also acquired one after Pollaiuolo, a Giuseppe Cesari, Luigi Bisi, and Murillo (lot. nos. 53, 60, 106, 112a). These are SN 451, 108, 16, 347, 271.

13 Undated cable of 3/29.

14 This was the sale of the Joseph Spiridon collection at Cassirer and Helbing.

15 Cable of 6/16/29.

16 Undated Cable of 6/29.

17 In the collection of her highness Princess Paley, widow of the Grand Duke Paul of Russia, by George Dawes were four portraits, lot. nos. 20-23 of tsars and tsarinas of Russia, the Hubert Roberts one of which was illustrated *Roman Buildings* and *The Bridge* lot nos. 40 and 41. *The Harpignies* was in the section of the sale from the Denys Hague collection and was probably lot no. 105.

18 Christie's sale June 28, 1929 lot no. 27. At the same time Ringling acquired a Valdes Leale *Salome* from the collection of Lord d'Abernon (SN 352) and a Moroni *Portrait* (SN 106). In addition cables to Böhler from Christie's indicate that on June 28 Ringling also purchased lot 25, a Teniers *Violinist* for £546.

19 Undated handwritten draft for a cable.

20 Cable of 7/12/29 the same day as the sale. The works referred to are the Albani (SN 21), Bourdon's set of the *Seven Acts of Mercy* (SN 366-372), Annibale *St. John the Baptiste* (SN114), Giordano *Mars and Venus*

(SN 160), Guercino *Annunciation* (SN 122), Maratta *Vision of a Saint* (SN 133) Molas (SN 138 and 139), Murillo (SN 351), Padovanino (SN 142), Poussin (SN 361), Reni *David and Goliath* (SN 117), Salome (SN 119), Rosa (SN 154) and also he acquired a Rosa *St. Jerome* (SN 151) and Tintoretto (SN 141). The Rembrandt a *Woman with Folded Arms* which like most of the others had been mentioned in Dr. Waagen's *Art Treasures in Great Britain*, was lot no. 75 and turned out to be a copy.

21 Cable of 26/8/29.

22 Cable of 12/9/29 and Weeks, 1993, p.218.

23 Cable of 14/9/29.

24 See Emile Moliniere, *Collection Emile Gavet, Catalogue Raisonné* (Paris, 1889), vol. I, p.186, no. 796 and vol. II, pl. LXXVIIII; and the exhibition catalougue *Niklaus Manuel Deutsch* (Kunstmuseum, Bern, 1979), pp. 223-224, nos. 69 and 70, pls. 30 and 32.

25 See, for example, cables of 28/2/30, 26/8/29, 5/3/30 and 18/3/30.

26 Cable of 2/5/30

27 Weeks, 1993, p.219.

28 Undated nightletter.

29 Cable of 7/10/30 from Ringling to Böhler and with Böhler's handwritten answer.

30 Cables of 22/8/30 and 26/9/30.

31 Nightletter of 29/10/30.

32 Cable of 4/11/30.

33 Cable of 3/1/31.

34 Letter of 1/6/31.

35 Cable of 20/2/31.

36 Cable of 24/2/31.

37 Weeks, 1993, p.213.

38 May 8, 1931.

39 Cable of 3/6/31.

40 Handwritten draft of 13/6/31.

41 Handwritten letter of 30/7/31.

42 Cable of 25/9/31.

43 Undated Nightletter.

44 Cable of 8/31.

45 Cable of 14/31.

46 Nightletter of 14/10/31.

47 Letter of 26/10/31.

48 Weeks, 1993, p.232.

49 Letter of 3/12/32.

50 Cable of x/x/32. On Ringling's physical and financial problems see Weeks, 1993, p.248.

51 Letter of 10/11/32.

52 Cable of 23/10/1933.

53 Letter of 10/11/32.

54 Letter of 3/3/35.

55 Letter of 7/15/35.

56 Letter of 8/1/36, one of the Deutsches was sold to the collector Oskar Reinhart of Wintherthur, Switzerland, who placed it on permanent deposit at the Kunstmuseum, Bern. See the catalogue *Niklaus Manuel Deutsch*. (Kunstmuseum, Bern, 1979), pp. 223-24.

In and Out of the Auction House: Collector to Connoisseur

1 Douglas and Eleanor Rigby, *Lock, Stock, and Barrel*. (New York: J. B. Lippincott Co., 1944), p. 83.

2 David C. Weeks, *Ringling: The Florida Years, 1911 - 1936*. (Gainesville: University of Florida Press, 1993), p. 313.

3 Julius W. Böhler. Julius W. Böhler Papers, "Sarasota Catalog," Ringling Museum Archives.

4 *Lock, Stock and Barrel*, p. 323.

5 *Sarasota Herald*, "John Ringling Sparing of Words But Tells of Plans for Art Museum." Tuesday, June 19, 1928. p.1.

6 When decorating Cà d'Zan, Mable did enlist the aid of a decorat-

ing firm but remained actively involved in the purchase of most pieces.

7 *Early American and British Portraits from the Frank Bulkeley Smith Collection.* April 17, 1920. JRAC, Ringling Museum Archives.

8 "Lessons of a Sale," *Art News*, May 1, 1920, p. 4.

9 W. G. Constable. *Art Collecting in the United States of America.* (London: Thomas Nelson and Sons, Ltd., 1964), p. 6.

10 "Albert Keller, 60, Hotel Leader, Dies," *New York Times*, October 23, 1939.

11 Julius W. Böhler Papers, Invoices - 1927, Ringling Museum Archives.

12 *Art News.* "Ringling Museum Will Be Open Next Winter." vol. 26, no. 31. May 5, 1928. p. 1-2.

13 *Ancient and Modern Pictures and Drawings from various sources; also Modern Pictures and Drawings, the property of J. W. Burnett, Esq., of Rock Hall...* Christies, London. May 23, 1928. JRAC Ringling Museum Archives.

14 *Literary Digest*, "Bidding in the Thousands." vol 90. 1926. p. 24.

15 At the time he wrote this article, Friedlander was already on the first board of directors of the Ringling Museum.

16 René Gimpel. *Diary of An Art Dealer, 1918-1939.* (New York: Universe Books, 1987), p. 352.

17 Christie's *Season 1931.* (London: Constable and Company Ltd., 1931), p. 39.

18 René Gimpel. *Diary of An Art Dealer, 1918-1939.* p. 359.

19 Lionello Venturi, "Private Collections of Italian Paintings." *Art in America,* vol 32, no. 4. October 1944, p. 170.

20 Julius W. Böhler Papers. Ringling Museum Archives.
21 John Ringling Papers, Ringling Museum Archives.
22 *The London Times.* July 5, 1924.
23 "Holford Sale," *The Art News.* August 20, 1927.
24 Christie's *Season 1929.* p. 24.
25 Christie's *Season 1930.*
26 Christie's *Season 1931.* p. 21.
27 The purchase as a *portrait of Philip IV* by Velasquez in 1912 by Henry Frick was considered "a new milestone" for the understanding of the artist among collectors. Wilhelm R. Valentiner, "Valentiner on American Art Collecting." *The Art News.* vol. xxv, no. 18. February 5, 1927.
28 *Sarasota Herald,* "John Ringling Sparing of Words But Tells of Plans for Art Museum." Tuesday, June 19, 1928. p.1.
29 Stephan Bourgeois, "The Passion of Art Collectors." *The Art News.* vol.xxxvi, no. 28, April 14, 1928. p. 63.
30 "Has John Ringling Regained Financial Power, Circus World?" *Every Week in Sarasota County.* August 30, 1935, p. 1.

A Collection of Baroque Masterpieces

1 Julius Böhler, "John Ringling Builder and Collector," in *The Art Museum John Ringling Built.,* (Sarasota, 1949), p. 15.
2 See Eric Zafran, "A History of Italian Baroque Painting in America," in *Botticelli to Tiepolo: Three Centuries of Italian Painting from Bob Jones University.* The Philbrook Museum of Art, (Tulsa, 1994).
3 René Brimo, *L'Evolution du Goût aux Etats-Unis,* (Paris, 1938), p. 122.
4 See Art Gallery, University of Notre Dame, *Handbook of the Collection.* (Notre Dame, 1967).
5 See Zafran, 1994, pp. 37-40.
6 See Detroit Institute of Arts, *Catalogue of Paintings....* (Detroit, 1920), pp. 7-12.
7 See Zafran, 1994, pp. 45-48.
8 See Burton Fredrickson, *Handbook of the Paintings in the Hearst San Simeon Historical Monument,* (1976).
9 See Federico Zeri, *Italian Paintings in the Walters Art Gallery,* (Baltimore, 1976), and Eric Zafran, "Introduction," *Fifty Old Master Paintings from the Walters Art Gallery,* (Baltimore, 1988), pp. 11-12.
10 "Ringling Museum will be open next Winter," *Art News,* XXVI, no. 31, May 5, 1928, p.2.
11 Letter in the Böhler-Ringling Archives of 3/14/29 sent from Sarasota to Lucerne. The book still in the Ringling library is by Giovanni Rosini published in Pisa, 1853.
12 From a cable of 7/12/29 from Ringling to Böhler.
13 Referred to in William H. Wilson, "John Ringling and the Flemish-Dutch Connection," in the catalogue of *The Flemish and Dutch Paintings, 1400-1900,* The John and Mable Ringling Museum of Art. (Sarasota, 1980), n.p.
14 See *A History of the Hispanic Society of America, Museum and Library, 1904-1954* (New York, 1957), pp.241-297.
15 "Ein Spätwerk Rembrandts, *Pantheon,* 1928, p. 160.
16 August Mayer, "Ribera in Ringling's Collection," *International Studio,* November 1929, pp.36-37.
17 The *Art Digest,* mid October 1930, vol.V, no.2, p.22.
18 W.R. Valentiner, "New Additions to the Work of Frans Hals," *Art in America,* XXIII, no. 3 (June 1935), p. 85.
19 Letter of 11/19/29 in the Ringling-Böhler correspondence.
20 See Wilson, 1980, n.p.
21 The *Exhibition of Italian Art of the Sei and Settecento* opened in Hartford in 1930.
22 William E. Suida, *Catalogue of Paintings, The John and Mable Ringling Museum of Art.* (Sarasota, 1949), pp. 1-2.
23 A. Hyatt Mayor, "The greatest show down south," *Art News,* XLVII, no.4, (Summer, June-August 1948), p.61.
24 *Art News Annual,* XIX, 1950, p.219.
26 W.G. Constable, *Art Collecting in the United States of America, An Outline of a History* (London, 1964), pp. 138-139.
27 Rudolph Wittkower and Frederick Cummings, *Art in Italy 1600-1700* (Detroit Institute of Arts, 1965).
28 Pierre Rosenberg, "Le musée de Sarasota en Floride," *L'Oeil,* no. 138, June 1966, pp.5-6.
29 Quoted in the *Baltimore Sun,* 1986.

The Library: The Education of a Connoisseur

1 John Ringling will, May 19, 1934.
2 The manuscript, apparently purchased by the Museum in 1982 and recently discovered in the curatorial files, is one of the few surviving written documents of the library in its early Gallery 20 location.
3 Conversation with Helen Strader,

March 26, 1996.

4 *Bulletin* (Sarasota, FL: School of Fine and Applied Art of the John and Mable Ringling Art Museum, 1931). p. 16.

5 Taylor Gordon, *Born to Be* , (New York: Covici-Friede Publishers, 1929), p. 145.

6 Gordon, p. 141.

7 This document is now in the Sarasota County Historical Archives.

8 The sale of Stillwell's library took place on December 5 and 6, 1927. Cunningham's books were auctioned on April 24 and 25, 1928.

9 The catalogue of this sale, which took place July 25-27, 1927, is in the Archives of The John and Mable Ringling Museum of Art. Its full title is: *Catalogue of the Valuable Library-The Property of Carpenter Garnier, Esq. Deceased; late of Rookesbury Park, Wickham, Hants and Works on the Fine Arts, Miscellaneous Books, Manuscripts and Autograph Letters, The Property of Dr. J.T. Langley, Mrs. B.W. Leader and F. B. Greenstreet, Esq. & Sir Edward Marshall Hall, K.C.*

10 E. Louise Lucas, *The Harvard List of Books on Art* , (Cambridge, MA: Harvard University Press, 1952), p. iii-iv.

11 Mary W. Chamberlain, *Guide to Art Reference Books* , (Chicago: American Library Association, 1959), p. 94.

12 Erwin Panofsky, quoted by Etta Arntzen and Robert Rainwater, *Guide to the Literature of Art History*, (Chicago: American Library Association, 1980), p. 328.

13 Arntzen and Rainwater, op. cit., p. 331.

14 Chamberlain, p. 72.

15 *Connoisseur*, 79, September 1927, p.3.

16 Chamberlain, p. 72.

17 *Connoisseur.*, 80, January 1928, p. 45.

18 Christie's *Season 1928* , (London: Constable & Co., 1928), p. 22-23.

19 The others, listed on the McGurk inventory, were C.G. Hartley's *A Record of Spanish Painting*; Christie's *Season 1929*; Bernete Y. Moret's *The School of Madrid; The Great Events by Famous Historians* and the Metropolitan Museum of Art—*Lists for a collection of casts.*

20 Chamberlain, op. cit., p. 270.

21 *In August Company: the Collections of the Pierpont Morgan Library*, (New York: Pierpont Morgan Library, 1993), p. 19.

22 Dale Roylance, *European Graphic Arts: the Art of the Book from Gutenberg to Picasso*, (Princeton: Princeton University, 1986), p. 9.

23 Conversation with Dr. David C. Weeks, March 25, 1996.

The Astor Rooms

Mr. Conforti wishes to thank Gene Ray for this edited adaptation of two lectures delivered at the Ringling Museum in 1984 and 1994 and Ann Friedman for her assistance with the initial research for this essay.

1 On the Astor house sale, see *The New York Times*, March 30, 1926, p. 10.

2 Often with the architect and interior designer Benjamin Wyatt as their interpretive link, George IV and his Tory friends—among them the Duke of Wellington, the Duke of York and the Marquess of Londonderry—regularly forsook the Gothic and classical fashions of the time in order to recall a French past barely 100 years old.

3 On the Louis Phillipe Rococo revival, see Carol Duncan, *The Pursuit of Pleasure: The Rococo Revival in French Romantic Art*, (New York and London, 1976); and Seymour O. Simches, *Le Romantisme et le Goût Esthétique du XVIIIe Siècle*, (Paris, 1964).

4 On Victorian interiors in the context of nineteenth century social history, see Kenneth L. Ames, "Meaning in Artifacts and Hall Furnishings in Victorian America," *Journal of Interdisciplinary History*, 9, (Summer 1978), pp. 19-46; and Clifford E. Clark, Jr., "Domestic Architecture as an Index to Social History: The Romantic Revival and the Cult of Domesticity in America, 1840-1870," *Journal of Interdisciplinary History*, 7, (Summer 1976), pp. 33-56.

5 On Caroline Astor's historical dressing, see Kate Simon, *A Very Social History*, (New York, 1978), p. 84. On Hunt, see Paul Baker, *Richard Morris Hunt, (* Cambridge and London), 1980.

6 For photographs of Hunt's W.K. Vanderbilt house, see John V. Van Pelt, *A Monograph of the William K. Vanderbilt House*, (New York, 1925).

7 See T. Gannon, *Newport Mansions: The Gilded Age*, (Little Compton, Rhode Island, 1982); and Montgomery Schuyler, "The Works of the Late Richard Morris Hunt," *The Architectural Record*, vol. 5, no. 2, October-December, 1895, pp. 97-180. Mr. Conforti thanks Paul Miller of the Preservation Society of Newport County for information on the artists and historical precedents of Marble House.

8 Much has been written on the rivalry and on other aspects of

Caroline Astor's 30 year tenure as New York's leading social arbiter. See, for example, Harvey O'Conner, *The Astors*, (New York, 1941), pp. 191-244 and the more accurate and less chatty Virginia Cowles, *The Astors*, (London, 1979), pp. 90-122.

9 Numerous drawings exist for the Astor House in the Hunt Collection at the American Institute for Architects Foundation in Washington, D.C., but no presentation drawing for the house as built has survived. I have proposed a chronology for all of the Astor House drawings which is on file at the archive.

10 For a discussion and photographs of the renovation, see "The Residence of Col. John Jacob Astor," *The Architectural Record* , 27, 1910, pp. 470-482.

11 For a contemporary description of the library, see *The New York Times*, December 6, 1925, p. 3.

12 The still-active social leader and philanthropist Brooke Astor was Vincent Astor's third wife.

13 See note 1. John Ringling was one of the most successful bidders at the sale, purchasing many paintings, the tapestries from the south dining room/library and, for $1,000, the paneling of Mr. Astor's reception room.

The Gavet-Vanderbilt-Belmont Collection

1 John Foreman and Robbe Pierce Stimson, *The Vanderbilts and the Gilded Age: Architectural Aspirations, 1879 - 1901*, (New York, 1991), p.222, attribute the design of the Gothic Room to Gilbert Cuel. David Chase, in "Superb Privacies: The Later Domestic Commissions of Richard Morris Hunt 1878 - 1895," in Susan R. Stein, ed., *The Architecture of Richard Morris Hunt*, (Chicago and London, 1986), p. 171, note 24, attributes the design of the Gothic Room to Moreau Frères based on two drawings in the Hunt archive, the American Institute of Architects Foundation, in Washington, D.C.:78.803 and 78.804.

2 Paul F. Miller, "The Gothic Room in Marble House, Newport, Rhode Island," *The Magazine Antiques,* Vol. CXLVI, no.2, August, 1994, p. 182.

3 Miller, 1994, p.186, n.9. It is important to mention in this context that an enameled terracotta relief of the Madonna and Child by Luca della Robbia was sold by Gavet to Henry G. Marquand between 1894 and 1897, presumably for his townhouse designed by Richard Morris Hunt at 8 East 68th Street in Manhattan. I would like to suggest that Allard was the broker/decorator in this case as well, serving as the link between Gavet and Hunt. This relief was sold in 1903 to Mrs. George T. Bliss, and eventually bequeathed to the Metropolitan Museum of Art by Susan Dwight Bliss in 1966 where it remains. On Marquand's house, see Paul R. Baker, *Richard Morris Hunt,* (Cambridge, MA, 1980), pp. 293 - 299.

4 In her novel based on the life of Alva Vanderbilt Belmont, Margaret Hayden Rector suggests that Gavet might have died shortly after the sale to the Vanderbilts due to his sadness at parting from his collection: *Alva, That Vanderbilt-Belmont Woman: Her story as she might have told it*, (Wickford, Rhode Island: The Dutch Island Press, 1992), p. 172.

5 James Maher, *Twilight of Splendor*, (Boston, 1975), p. 57. The name of the firm was Allard & Sons and Prignot. Alavoine, another firm, opened in New York in 1893, and in 1905 bought out Allard's business.

6 Maher, p. 57. Herter directed one of the most important decorating firms in America. See the catalogue *Herter Brothers:Furniture and Interiors for a Gilded Age,* Katherine S. Howe et. al., (New York, 1994).

7 Maher (p.59) points out that, director of the American partnership of Alavoine, Edouard Hitau, also served as a consultant to the Metropolitan Museum of Art in New York for the installation of two period rooms which were to have been placed in the New York mansion of Mrs. Hubert N. Straus.

8 Colin Simpson, *Artful Partners: Bernard Berenson and Joseph Duveen*, (New York, 1986), p. 278.

9 Foreman and Stimson, p.221.

10 Quoted in Foreman and Stimson, p. 227.

11 On Böhler, see David C. Weeks, *Ringling: The Florida Years, 1911-1936*, (Gainesville, Florida: The University of Florida Press, 1993).

12 Maher, p. 136.

13 Peter Tomory, *Catalogue of the Italian Paintings before 1800*, (Sarasota: The John and Mable Ringling Museum of Art, 1976), p. 14.

Bibliography

"Albert Keller, 60, Hotel Leader, Dies." *The New York Times*, Monday, October 23, 1939.

"American and British Art Buyers Again Clinch," *Literary Digest*. 73: 29-30, 1922.

"The American Collector of Antiques." *Arts and Decoration*. 27:35-6, 1927.

"The American Opportunity," *Arts and Decoration*. 16: 288-9. 1922.

Arntzen, Etta and Robert Rainwater. *Guide to the Literature of Art History*. Chicago: American Library Association, 1980.

"Aspects of British Collecting, Part I." Denys Sutton. *Apollo*. November 1981. pp. 282-328. Part II, December 1982, pp. 358-405.

Baker, Paul R., *Richard Morris Hunt*, Cambridge, MA, 1980.

Basbanes, Nicholas A. *A Gentle Madness: Bibliophiles, Bibliomanes, and the Eternal Passion for Books*. New York: Holt, 1995.

"Bidding in the Thousands," *Literary Digest*. 90:24, 1926. p. 24.

Bourgeois, Stephen. "The Passion of Art Collectors." *The Art News*. vol xxxvi, no. 28. April 14, 1928. p. 63-65.

Brimo, René. Art et Gout: *L'Évolution du Goût Aux États-Unis: D'Après des Collections*. James Fortune: Paris. 1938.

Bulletin. School of Fine and Applied Art of the John and Mable Ringling Museum. Sarasota, FL, 1931.

Bureau of Historic Sites and Properties. *Historical, Architectural, and Archaeological Survey of Sarasota*. Project Series #51, 1982.

Burt, Nathaniel. *Palaces for the People: A Social History of the American Art Museum*. Boston: Little, Brown and Company, 1977.

Catalogue des Tableaux Anciens et Quelques Modernes... Provenant de la Collection de feu M. Emile Gavet, Hotel Drouot, Paris, 1906.

Chamberlain, Mary W. *Guide to Art Reference Books*. Chicago: American Library Association, 1959.

"Changing Tastes in Picture Collecting." *The International Studio*. vol. LXXXII, No. 346. March 1926. p. 48-54.

Chase, David, "Superb Privacies: The Later Domestic Commissions of Richard Morris Hunt 1878 - 1895," in Susan R. Stein, ed., *The Architecture of Richard Morris Hunt*, Chicago and London, 1986.

"Collective Genius: the Importance of the Walters Art Gallery." *Connoisseur*. 873: 148-151, 1984.

Constable, W. G. *Art Collecting in the United States of America: An Outline of a History*. Thomas Nelson and Sons, Ltd.: London. 1964.

Cordner, Frank. "The Ringling Museum of Art," in the *Florida Architect*. September/October, 1970.

Cortissoz, Royal. "The American Collector of Antiques." *Arts & Decoration*. vol. XXVII, no. 1. May 1927. p. 35-6.

Curl, Donald W. *Mizner's Florida: American Resor Architecture*. New York: The Architectural History Foundation, 1984.

Carter, A. C. R. *Let Me Tell You*. Hutchinson & Co.: London. date?

Duncan Philips: Centennial Exhibition. Philips Collection. Washington, D.C. 1986.

Duval, Cynthia and Karcheski, Walter J., Jr., *Medieval and Renaissance Splendor: Arms and Armor from the Higgins Armory Museum, Worcester, Massachusetts, and Works of Art from the John and Mable Ringling Museum of Art, Sarasota, Florida*, Exhibition Catalogue, 1983.

Foreman John and Stimson, Robbe Pierce, *The Vanderbilts and the Gilded Age: Architectural Aspirations, 1879 - 1901*, New York, 1991.

Freitag, Wolfgang. *Art Books: a Basic Bibliography of Monographs on Artists.* New York: Garland Publishing, Inc., 1985.

Gimpel, René. *Diary of An Art Dealer, 1918-1939.* Universe Books: New York. 1987.

"Holford Italian Paintings." *The Art News.* August 20, 1927.

Hoving, Thomas. *False Impressions: The Hunt for Big-Time Art Fakes.* Simon & Schuster: New York, 1996.

Howey, John. *The Sarasota School of Architecture.* Cambridge, Massachusetts: The MIT Press, 1995.

Janson, Anthony F. *Great Paintings from the John and Mable Ringling Museum of Art.* Sarasota: The John and Mable Ringling Museum of Art, 1986.

Levarie, Norma. *The Art and History of Books.* New Castle, DE: Oak Knoll Press, 1995.

"Lesson of a Sale." *American Art News.* May 1, 1920. p. 4.

Lloyd, David. "Changing Tastes in Picture Collecting." *The International Studio.* Vol. LXXXIII, No. 346. March 1926. p. 48-54.

"The Lure of the Auction." *Country Life.* 50: 45, 1937.

Maher, James, *Twilight of Splendor,* Boston, 1975.

Miller, Paul F., "The Gothic Room in Marble House, Newport, Rhode Island," *The Magazine Antiques,* Vol. CXLVI, no.2, August, 1994, p. 176 - 185.

Molinier, Emile, *Catalogue de Collection Timbal...,* Paris, 1882.

_____, and Courajod, Louis, *Donation de Baron Charles Daviller,* Paris, 1885.

_____,*Collection Emile Gavet,* Paris, 1889.

_____,*Catalogue des Objets d'Art et de Haute Curiosit, de la Renaissance. Tableaux, Tapisseries composant la collection de M. Emile Gavet et dont le vente aura lieu Galerie Georges Petit...Du Lundi 31 Mai au Mercredi 9 Juin 1897.*

_____,"Le Museé, du mobilier Français au Louvre," Gazette des Beaux Arts, Vol. 25, 1901.

"Money In Masterpieces." *Literary Digest.* vol. 102. September 28, 1929. p. 19.

Rector, Margaret Hayden, Alva, *That Vanderbilt-Belmont Woman: Her story as she might have told it,* Wickford, Rhode Island: The Dutch Island Press, 1992.

Reitlinger, Gerald. *The Economics of Taste: The Rise and Fall of Picture Prices 1790-1960.* Vols I - III. Hacker Art Books: New York. 1982.

Rigby, Douglas and Elizabeth. *Lock, Stock, and Barrel.* J.B. Lippincott Co.: New York. 1944.

"Ringling Museum Will Be Open Next Winter." *The Art News.* vol. xxxvi, no. 31. May 5, 1928, p. 1-2.

Robinson, Franklin W. and William H. Wilson. *The Flemish and Dutch Paintings, 1400-1900.* Sarasota: The John and Mable Ringling Museum of Art, 1980.

Robinson, John Martin. "The Ruin of the Historic English Collections." *Connoisseur.* 805: March 1979. pp. 162-16.

Roylance, Dale. *European Graphic Arts: the Art of the Book from Gutenberg to Picasso.* Princeton: Princeton University, 1986.

"The Sale Room: Duke of Westminster's Pictures." *The London Times.* July 5, 1924.

Saarinen, Aline. *The Proud Possessors: The Lives, Times, and Tastes of Some Adventuous American Art Collectors.* New York: Random House, 1959.

Schmidt, Valentine L. *Rare Books of the 16th, 17th and 18th Centuries from the Library of the Ringling Museum of Art, Sarasota, Florida,* 1969.

Seligman, Germain. *Merchants of Art: 1880-1960; Eighty Years of Professional Collecting*. Appleton: New York. 1961.

Simpson, Colin, *Artful Partners: Bernard Berenson and Joseph Duveen*, New York, 1986.

Smith, Elizabeth Bradford, et. al. *Medieval Art in America: Patterns of Collection, 1800-1940*. University Park, Pennsylvania: The Palmer Museum of Art, 1996.

Spiess, Philip D. II. "Toward a New Professionalism: American Museums in the 1920s and 1930s," in *Museum News*, vol. 75, no. 2 (March/April 1996), pp.38-47.

Suida, William. *Catalogue of Paintings in the John and Mable Ringling Museum of Art*. Sarasota: The John and Mable Ringling Museum of Art, 1949.

Suida, William. "Three Newly Identified Paintings in the Ringling Museum." *Art in America*. Vol. 32, no. 1. January 1944. pp.5-11.

Tomory, Peter, *Catalogue of the Italian Paintings before 1800*, The John and Mable Ringling Museum of Art, 1976.

Valentiner. Wilhelm R. "Valentiner on American Collecting." *The Art News*. Vol. XXV, No. 18. February 5, 1927. p. 1-7.

Venturi, Lionello. "Private Collections of Italian Paintings." *Art in America*. vol. 32, no. 4. p. 168-177.

Vilas, C.N. and N.R. *The John and Mable Ringling Museum of Art, A Guide to the Collection*. Chicago: Heller, 1942.

Walker, John. *Self-Portrait with Donors: Confessions of an Art Collector*. Little, Brown and Company: Boston. 1974.

Watts, Harvey M. "The American Opportunity." *Arts and Decoration*. vol. 16. February 9, 1922. pp. 288-289.

Weeks, David C. *Ringling: The Florida Years, 1911-1936*. Gainesville, Florida: The University Press of Florida, 1993.

Wyer, Raymond. "Permanent Collections for Small Museums." *The International Studio*. Vol. LVI, No. 221. July 18, 1916. p. xxxiii-xxxix.

Index of Artists